DAVID DAICHES is Professor of English and Dean of the School of English and American Studies at the University of Sussex. Educated at Edinburgh University, and with a D. Phil. from Oxford, he has taught English at Edinburgh, Oxford, Chicago, Cornell, Indiana, Cambridge, and the Sorbonne. He is the author of some twenty books, including *The Novel and the Modern World; Robert Burns, A Critical History of English Literature,* and works on Virginia Woolf, Robert Louis Stevenson, and George Eliot. He is also one of the editors of *The Norton Anthology of English Literature.*

A STUDY OF LITERATURE

For Readers and Critics

DAVID DAICHES

The Norton Library

W · W · NORTON & COMPANY · INC ·

NEW YORK

≫ W. W. Norton & Company, Inc. is also the publisher of
The Norton Anthology of English Literature, edited by M. H.
Abrams, Robert M. Adams, David Daiches, E. Talbot Donaldson,
George H. Ford, Samuel Holt Monk, and Hallett Smith; *The
American Tradition in Literature,* edited by Sculley Bradley, Rich-
mond Croom Beatty, and E. Hudson Long; *World Masterpieces,*
edited by Maynard Mack, Kenneth Douglas, Howard E. Hugo,
Bernard M. W. Knox, John C. McGalliard, P. M. Pasinetti,
and René Wellek; *The Norton Reader,* edited by Arthur M.
Eastman, Caesar R. Blake, Hubert M. English, Jr., Alan B. Howes,
Robert T. Lenaghan, Leo F. McNamara, and James Rosier; and
the NORTON CRITICAL EDITIONS, in hardcover and paperbound:
authoritative texts, together with the leading critical interpretations,
of major works of British, American, and Continental literature.

Preface to a New Edition

IN THE seventeen years since I wrote this book I have of course changed my mind about a number of things discussed in it, but not about any matter of substance. The more I read and think about and talk about literature the more dubious I become of fixed categories and text-book definitions and the more important it seems to me to expose oneself to the reality and variety of literary works themselves. At the same time, I do not for a moment believe that an inquiry into the nature and value of works of imaginative literature is a barren theoretical activity of no interest to those whose concern is to read and enjoy literary works. To know why we enjoy and value something is often to increase the enjoyment and enhance the valuation: nearly thirty years of teaching English at universities have left me in no doubt of that. It is also true that intelligent people *like* to reflect on the meaning and value of what they read. Man is an inquiring animal, and anyone who has read and enjoyed a poem easily becomes interested in and even excited by the question, "What is a poem?" Since an endeavor to answer such a question inevitably leads the inquirer back to particular poems, it is wrong to say that the kind of general inquiry I try to conduct in this book takes people away from the actual reading of literary works. Illustration, comparison, description, analysis, detailed references of all kinds to individual works, are inevitably involved once we embark on the kind of discussion represented here. The question "Why read a book?" involves the question "What is a book?" It was because the question "How to read a book?" was being so loudly discussed in the 1940's with no reference to "Why?" and "What?" that I originally decided to make this study.

A reviewer of the original edition, taking literally the remark I made in the opening sentence of the Preface, accused me of cruelty to students (and also of critical naiveté) in stopping them as they streamed out of a classroom to ask them why they bothered to read works telling of events which never occurred. I should perhaps confess now that this was a mere rhetorical gambit. I never in fact hung around the exits of classrooms and lecture halls ready to pounce on students of literature with that question. In pretending that I did, I was merely trying to highlight the paradox that students were being trained in highly sophisticated techniques of literary analysis without being encouraged (in some cases being actively discouraged) to reflect on why the works analyzed were worth taking to pieces in that way at all. For much of the critical analysis done then, as now, never emerged with anything to suggest why the original work was *valuable*. Of course one might say, as many English critics say, that we all know as a matter of common sense what the value of a work of literature is for us. But modern American academic criticism has moved so far beyond common sense, and has taught so many students to distrust any first common-sense reaction to a literary work, that they often no longer have common sense to fall back on. The critical discussion of literature becomes a sophisticated game with fixed rules and a special terminology, and the student who wants academic advancement learns to play it. The results can be disastrous: we all know academic scholars and critics who read good works of literature only when they have an article to write or a competitive point to make or a class to teach, and in the privacy of their own homes read "for pleasure" (or "to relax") an ephemeral detective story.

So I think that it is important, particularly at this moment in the history of the academic teaching of literature, to ask what it is all about, what it is all *for,* and to try to answer the question in such a way as to relate the question of value to the question of how we describe and analyze a literary work. This book is not an essay in abstract aesthetics, nor (in spite of the fact that I have been reproached with using the word "epistemology" on the first page) is it primarily philosophical. It is primarily *critical,* and its objective is to bring together two different kinds of critical inquiry: that into the nature and value of literature and that into the most effective way of establishing whether it is good.

I claim no finality for my observations, some of which I would put quite differently if I were writing the book today. The title is perhaps misleading in that it suggests a comparison with Arnold Toynbee's monumental *Study of History.* My study of literature is more limited and more tentative, meant to suggest lines of thought and response rather than to establish a system. (I had originally intended to call the book "Why Read a Book?" — but my friends urged that this was a slick, catch-penny title that would attract the wrong sort of reader. They may have been right;

but that title accurately expressed my purpose in writing it.)

The more sophisticated critics of our time suspect and even resist this kind of book. One reviewer even resented my intelligibility: serious critical writing ought to be less easy to read than this, he thought. Another reproached me for my common sense and for taking the "middle road" instead of championing some exotic heresy. This sort of reaction confirmed my belief in the necessity of this sort of book. Not that I would for a moment claim that I have done the job particularly well (I am very conscious of the book's faults after all these years); but I am sure it is the kind of job that ought to be done.

Reading again in 1964 what I wrote in 1947, I have become aware of certain stresses, certain pressures of particular interests in the book, that reflect not only books but also nonliterary issues that I was concerned with at the time. Every book that represents any genuine thought at all must reflect the personal intellectual and emotional history of the writer, and it does not seem to me now that the resulting emphases produce anything that I should wish away. But perhaps I ought to explain that the defensive tone of the final two paragraphs came about because I wrote the last chapter after a long discussion the previous night with a colleague especially interested in the developing countries of Africa and Asia: the discussion weighed heavily on my mind as I wrote the conclusion. The course of history in the last seventeen years has not made it any less relevant, and though again I might not put the matter exactly in this way if I were writing today, I think it can stand.

Falmer, Sussex
August, 1964   D.D.

Contents

Preface

SOME TIME AGO, as I watched a crowd of students swarm out of a classroom where they had been listening to a lecture on the technique of the novel, it occurred to me to approach one of them and ask him this simple question: "Why do you spend time reading and discussing books which tell of events which never in fact occurred?" He was understandably taken aback by my sudden questioning, but even when he had recovered from his first surprise he proved unable to give an answer that satisfied either himself or me. I tried the experiment on some others, with the same result. Yet they were all students who had learned to talk skillfully about character and plot and fiction, about different technical devices used by different novelists, about description and dialogue, foreshadowing and climax, and all the other things that analysis of the fiction writer's art has taught us to be concerned about. Faced with the elementary question about the ultimate purpose of it all, they had no answer.

My question was, of course, elementary; but, as my experience proved, it is the elementary questions that are most easily taken for granted and never answered. It is a long time since Aristotle tried to explain the nature of poetic truth and its difference from the truth of history. Today most critics are more concerned with technique than with the basic question of value. There are any number of books which inquire into the structure of the novel, which discuss problems of characterization and plotting and try to explain what the work is in terms of what the author appears to have done. I am not here trying to enter into competition with such books, nor am I implying that they are not useful. All discussion is useful which helps us to clarify our ideas about the nature of works of literature. My own efforts are directed primarily toward the solution of a problem which seems to me to underlie all the others, a problem whose solution the others must assume. That problem can be most simply summed up in the question I put to the students of the technique of the novel: Why read a work of imaginative literature?

I do not delude myself that I can give any final answer to this question. But I do believe that it is useful to return periodically to a consideration of the use and value of literature, to leave for a while the more detailed technical discussion of the kinds of skill the writer must employ, and ask ourselves what, in the light of what we know about books and the reasons why they are read, can now be said in answer to the age-old charge that poets (by which is meant all writers of imaginative literature) are reprehensible because they tell lies. Can we accept any of the great classical answers, or must they be modified or discarded in the light of subsequent literary history? Can we agree on the *use* of imaginative literature, or must we take the defeatist course of praising it just because it has no use? The following pages represent one attempt to answer these questions as well as some related questions that I found it impossible to dissociate from them.

This book is not, however, intended as a purely theoretical contribution to aesthetics. Its main purpose is to help the reader of works of imaginative literature to see what he is reading, to understand just what it is that he gets from different kinds of reading, and to discriminate between those different kinds. I have tried to express myself as simply and cogently as I could, avoiding the jargon of any special school of criticism. I do not believe that it is the duty of a professor of English to write only for his colleagues or for those who share his views. The audience I have in mind is a sort of ideal "common reader"—but I hope that he does not prove too ideal, and that there are real examples of his kind.

It remains for me to render acknowledgment to Professor Max Schoen and the Philosophical Library, Inc., editor and publisher respectively of *The Enjoyment of the Arts,* for permission to use some paragraphs from a discussion of poetry which I contributed to that collection of essays.

Ithaca, New York
January, 1948

CHAPTER I

Problems of the Modern Critic

LITERATURE has been produced since long before people began to worry about its nature and value, and there is something to be said for the naïveté which enjoys art without asking questions about it. But civilized man cannot afford innocence: there comes a stage at which he must be prepared to justify all the activities which he considers significant or risk their surrender to the claims of morality, science, or efficiency. The subtler and less easily definable kinds of value are the most difficult to defend, for man is a political animal and political animals are not readily roused to the support of what cannot be expressed in slogans. Man is also a moral animal, and he has a liking for systems; and moral systems tend to be inflexible, to ignore what cannot be neatly fitted in, to suspect activities whose nature cannot be precisely defined. What exactly is it that a poet does? Plato was not the only one who approached this question in a previously determined moral context and after he had already made up his mind about a theory of knowledge. As a result, he came to the conclusion that poetry was a bad thing both on moral grounds (because it "nourishes the passions instead of controlling them") and on epistemological grounds (because the kind of knowledge which the poet communicates is not knowledge of reality but the observation of mere imitations of reality). There is a lot to be said for the Platonic view, and it has been held, consciously or otherwise, by a great variety of thoughtful people in many different ages. It reflects the growing claims of morality and science, and shows that, if you approach poetry *after* the claims of morality and science have been allowed, you have a hard time defending poetry even if (like Plato) you feel instinctively that it is both significant and valuable. The other way is not to define the claims of morality and science until all your data are in—and include the fact of the production and enjoyment of poetry among your data.

There is a second way of answering Plato, and that is to construct an epistemology in terms of which the kind of knowledge which poetry communicates can be seen as closer to reality rather than farther away from it. Aristotle can perhaps be said to have done this in his *Poetics,* when he replied to Plato by explaining that a poet is concerned with presenting individual things in such a way that their typical aspects are made clear (the typical being held to be more real than the specific)—an explanation which was not, in fact, inconsistent with Plato's own epistemology, which involved his famous theory of ideas; but Plato was prevented from using his own epistemology in this way by the fact that he had too much of his moral scheme already constructed by the time he came to discuss poetry in his *Republic.* (A very different and independently conceived theory of poetry is to be found in Plato's *Ion.*)

The Aristotelian view, however modified, has been the basis of most subsequent theories of poetry in the Western world. It is essentially a defense of poetry based on the kind of knowledge it communicates. Even Wordsworth, for all his insistence that "the end of poetry is to produce excitement in co-existence with an overbalance of pleasure" and his definition of poetry as "the spontaneous overflow of powerful feelings," is in the Aristotelian tradition when he says (in the same essay) that the poet "converses with general nature" and that "poetry is the breath and finer spirit of all knowledge." Imaginative literature, the formal presentation in language of what may not be literally true or true in the simplest scientific sense, has most often been defended because it embodies a kind of knowledge which cannot be expressed in any other way; it does this while giving a kind of pleasure which is similarly unique, and this knowledge and this pleasure are of such a nature as to enrich the personality of him who receives it.

Is this a valid line of defense? Looking round on the vast quantity of imaginative literature which the Western world has up till now accumulated, are we prepared to say that its value for us lies in its enrichment of our personalities by a unique knowledge and a unique pleasure? Is this why we read novels, poems, and plays? Is this what they in fact do for us? Do we perhaps want to draw a distinction between "classics" and our more casual reading? And what about literature as an activity of our own civilization? The fact that any such generalization as that with which the previous paragraph concludes makes us uncomfortable surely deserves examination.

We are uncomfortable, in the first place, because we want immediately to draw distinctions. A theory of literature which would apply to Homer and Shakespeare cannot, we feel, apply to the short story we read in this week's magazine—not because the short story is necessarily *less good,*

3

but because it is so completely different. The feeling that *Hamlet* and a modern Broadway play are incommensurable or, more definitely, that Homer and Sinclair Lewis, say, had completely different objectives and were doing quite different things must be fairly general. Generalizations about the use and value of literature do not interest us. What literature are we discussing?

Now this attitude does not arise from any suspicion of generalizations, because in other fields (the political, for example) the present age is probably more prone to generalization than any period in the past. It arises rather from a profound sense of the difference between modern literature and the classics of the past and from an awareness of the great differences in the nature, purpose, and value of the various kinds of "literary" works produced even in our own day. Is this a serious or a commercial writer? This is a very modern question. It is a question that Homer would certainly not and Shakespeare probably not have understood.

Our literature is very different from past literature and it represents a variety of quite different literary purposes; this would probably be maintained by most contemporaries who have thought of the matter at all. It is a quite new attitude. It never occurred to seventeenth- or eighteenth-century writers that they were doing something that differed substantially from what had been done by the writers of Greece and Rome. When Pope advised authors to follow Homer and Virgil, he was simply indicating his awareness of the fact that literary artists of all periods have had a common purpose, and any budding writer can therefore learn from any other successful practitioner, ancient or modern. What has happened to make the modern attitude so different?

One thing that has happened is the development of mass

education. In earlier ages ability to read was confined to a relatively small number of people, most of whom were anxious to use that ability in order to inform or enlighten themselves. The masses of the people were left to receive such information and enlightenment as those readers of books who were preachers or propagandists thought fit to communicate verbally. Such illiteracy has its compensations. It is good for the memory and strengthens the imagination. People who depend entirely on oral tradition will tend to cultivate an ear for the memorable and a taste for figures of speech. They will share in a folk literature and play their part in perpetuating and enlarging it. They will feel themselves to be participators in whatever art they have access to. Though they may not have access to the greatest literature, at least they will be custodians of an art that comes home to their business and bosoms, and within the limits of that art they will recognize and encourage integrity and vitality.

But one does not have to romanticize illiteracy in order to realize the modern problem. An industrial society which provides for everybody the technique of reading but is indifferent to the purpose to which reading is put by the vast numbers whom it has made *merely* literate is running some very serious risks. Reading involves the ability to receive communication from sources outside one's own immediate sphere; it puts no limits to the number of sources from which readers can receive facts and fancies, truths and lies, enlightenment and corruption. The invention of the alphabet made this possible, the invention of printing made it practicable on a large scale, and the invention of modern publishing made it inevitable. Reading is obviously the means to a great number of ends: it can be used for good or evil. Today the means is inevitable while the definition of the end is optional. Put that fact together with the further fact that modern publishing is a purely commercial operation, and there lies at least one part of the explanation of the unique modern attitude to literature.

The gap between "high-brow" and "popular" literature, which is closely bound up with the problem we are discussing and which is the source of so much confusion on the question of the nature of literary value, is one of the most obvious of contemporary cultural phenomena. The difference between readers in these two categories is not necessarily one of intelligence. True literacy is not a degree of intelligence or even a degree of skill, but a state of mind and imagination, which is possible at almost any intellectual level. Most young children are more literate in this sense than their elders, for their minds and imaginations have not yet been atrophied by lengthy exposure to dead stereotypes. The semiliteracy of the atrophied mind that can read only passively is bound to grow progressively farther away from adequate literacy since such a mind is only further atrophied by further reading. We have, in fact, to deal with three stages—illiteracy, semiliteracy, and true literacy—and as soon as we face the facts we realize that the first and the third have more in common than either has with the second.

In an age when reading for most people is a nonintellectual pleasure, and when at the same time there is a constant stream of books falling from the publishers' presses, a book has only to be barely readable once in order to serve its purpose. It need not be reread, nor does it need to lie in the mind as a source of future pleasure. It thus ceases to matter whether a book is memorable; and when literature is not memorable it is nothing. Total illiterates who depend on folk literature for their pleasures of the imagination are thus much better off than semiliterates who read forgettable novels merely because they are available. Oral literature must lie in the mind, for otherwise it would be forgotten; but most modern written literature is expected to be forgotten, in order to make way for the next season's list. That is one reason why we feel that modern books are different in kind from "the classics."

The fact is that literacy itself is a means and not an end, and it can be put to uses which may be good, bad, or indifferent. A book may be read for a great variety of reasons. But the reason for which a book is read determines the way it is read and to some extent the degree of illumination it is possible to get from it. All books should, of course, be read for pleasure, but "pleasure" is not a helpful term here, for it has so many meanings. There are many kinds of pleasure, intellectual and nonintellectual, and even many kinds of intellectual pleasures. The appreciation of literature involves a very special kind of intellectual pleasure, in which the intellectual element is not always directly manifested and where the faculty which critics have come to call the imagination plays a complicated and not always definable part. The ability to read does not by itself guarantee the ability to enjoy that kind of pleasure; it has, in fact, no particular connection with it at all except that it provides the technique for communicating it to those in a position to receive it. Like patriotism, literacy is not enough.

The organization of writers and critics into cliques and coteries, the disintegration of the artist's public not only into "high-brow" and "low-brow" but into all sorts of special groups and mutually contemptuous *salons,* reflect the

7

varied functions now being served by the ability to read. And this is to ignore books which are concerned simply with communicating facts or theories or which preach or prophesy or which attempt to be anything except what is now so often known as "creative writing." Imaginative literature, "poetry" in the old and wider sense of the word, is itself so divided in the purposes it serves and the audience it addresses that any modern poetics must be in part a work of sociology—either that or it must ignore the great bulk of literature and talk about literature not as it is but as it should be.

Aristotle's *Poetics* is a discussion of the nature and value of literature based on Greek literature as Aristotle found it. It is descriptive before it is evaluative and goes, with what sometimes seems to us unnecessary detail, into contemporary practice. Having defined literature in this way, he was able to point out its use and value. The modern critic cannot deal with literary phenomena so neatly. Has he an alternative which will not take him too far afield? The question in fact almost becomes the apparently silly but in fact very shrewd one: Is literary criticism still possible?

The answer to such a question can only be that literary criticism is possible if we distinguish the functions served by literature more sharply than Aristotle found it necessary to do. Aristotle's distinction between poetry and history— the former being more philosophical and more serious because more universal in its implications—remains fundamental, but it must remain in the background until we have examined not only the various ways in which writers today have given literary treatment to imaginary situations but also the different motives with which readers approach the resulting works. It is not necessary to concern oneself with

the social, economic, and other causes underlying these motives, or with the motives which impel writers to cater to the
tastes thus developed, in order to be able both to grade the
value of the motives and assess the works produced in response to them. But distinction between motives—which of
course means distinction between functions—is imperative.
It may of course be found that in many cases works which
ostensibly fulfill one function do in fact fulfill another as
well, but this is not an exclusively modern problem: many
past works are enjoyed today for reasons which would have
astonished their authors. In the past such problems have
been mainly concerned with the relation between the moral
(or didactic) and the aesthetic aspects of literature. Milton
did in fact write *Paradise Lost* to justify the ways of God to
men, and we appreciate it today without much regard for
this purpose. Today the main problem concerns not the
relation between the moral and the aesthetic, but that between entertainment value and aesthetic value. The vast
majority of books today are intended simply to entertain:
to what extent is their function as entertainment compatible
with their value as "literature"? ("Literature" is here put
in quotation marks to indicate that the term at this stage
of the argument is question-begging, as is "aesthetic"; for
what we have to discover is precisely what we mean by literary value *as such*.)

Whatever literary value may be, there can be little doubt
that it often exists in a work irrespective of its author's main
intention—or at least of his superficial intention. This presumably was a thought which never occurred to Aristotle,
but it is a most important thought for us, because it may
lead us to a point where we can ignore differences in ostensible function by pointing to a common "literary" or

"aesthetic" value existing in works produced for all sorts of reasons and for all sorts of audiences. This, however, is not an easy way out of our difficulty because today the majority of books written (and we are still talking about imaginative literature) do not seem to have any value in common with the great works of the past. Nevertheless, a substantial minority of such works do have such value, in some degree, even though their superficial functions may differ. Others have value, but not one which we can call literary value if that term also is to denote what we find in significant earlier literature. The first object, therefore, of the distinction between functions is to separate literary from non-literary value, and only after we have done that can we talk with any meaning about books being "good" or "bad." We can then come to a stage at which we may see that *value depends on real and not on apparent function*. And the real functions of works which can be classified as literature are strictly limited.

A novel may be written in order to bring home to its readers the true situation in, say, contemporary China. Its function, therefore, might be called merely informative, or journalistic. The facts might be written up in such a way as to induce a certain attitude in the reader, even make him incline to certain action; in which case its more fundamental function would be rhetorical—that is, it would seek to convince or persuade rather than to illuminate. While retaining its journalistic and rhetorical functions it might, however, also have a value as an illumination of an aspect of human experience, or as a carefully patterned and for that reason pleasing presentation of a linked series of events, or as something else whose appreciation does not depend on any interest on the reader's part in the information as information, or in the rhetoric as an inducement to adopt a certain attitude or take certain action. This would represent some kind of literary value, and if it was significant enough to give the book vitality apart from its journalistic or rhetorical aspects, its presentation might be called the book's real function. And this value would therefore be the book's true value—irrespective of the proportion of readers who may read it for its journalistic or its rhetorical function.

Is the literary critic concerned with all "good books" whatever the kind of goodness involved? Or is he concerned only with this last kind of value? Clearly, the book reviewer must concern himself with every kind of virtue which a book may possess. But the function of the literary critic differs from that of the reviewer, for the latter distinguishes between functions in order to discover why he should praise the book under consideration, while the former makes the distinction in order to decide whether it can be praised as literature. The reviewer can praise a telephone directory for what it is, but the literary critic has nothing to say about it. However, if the telephone directory were presented as literature, if its authors or publishers claimed that it was a literary work, then of course the literary critic would have to examine those claims and show that they were invalid. It is easy to see this in the case of the telephone directory, where the confusion between a literary and a nonliterary purpose is hardly conceivable; but there are cases where there is such a confusion, where a book has a nonliterary value but is presented as possessing a literary one, and there the reviewer may well praise the book for adequately fulfilling its nonliterary function (giving information about contemporary China, say, under the guise of "fiction") while the literary critic, ignoring its nonliterary claims, will assess it and condemn it on the basis of its false pretensions. On the other hand, a book may claim to be serving wholly and only a nonliterary purpose, and the critic may find that it is, nevertheless, serving a literary one.

Whichever way we turn, we are forced back to a definition of "literary purpose." If the combination of universal ability to read and modern publishing techniques has produced a welter of books claiming to be literature but in fact serving a great variety of purposes, and has also brought about the disintegration of the reading public and created an impassable gulf between "high-brow" and "low-brow," we can only bring order into our critical perceptions if we keep looking for a purpose and a value which, while they may coexist with other purposes and values, are, in the first place, unique (that is, not discoverable except in this kind of literary expression) and, in the second place, akin in kind if not in degree to those purposes and values which we recognize in memorable literary works of the past. If we find purposes and values which satisfy the first but not the second criterion, we *may* be on the track of a new kind of literary value, but we must look carefully before we conclude that what we see represents both a genuine value and a really new kind of value.

Let us begin our investigation by inquiring briefly into the reasons why people read books which are popularly known as "literature." It is hardly an exaggeration to say that most people read because they have nothing better to do. They read to escape boredom, to pass the time, or to escape into a world of wish fulfillment or excitement in which they can forget about the petty and often sordid details of a dull and unheroic life. Modern society has evolved many new ways of providing for the individual the means of supplying his economic wants; it has specialized in the *means* but done little about the end; it has created leisure but discovered no use for leisure, so that for many reading has become a method of filling in the leisure so arduously created. One works in order to give oneself the opportunity of not having to work; but what is one to do when there is no work to be done, except find some way of making the hours pass until it is time to work again? Thus the escapist aim is more prominent among readers of books today than ever before. Such an aim is not necessarily contemptible: its value depends on what one is escaping from and where one is escaping to. And there is nothing wrong in trying to forget some of the unpleasanter aspects of living in entertainment. But to forget things because they are unpleasant is not the same as to forget them because they are simply there and one does not know what to do with them. If one conceives of the function of work as to produce leisure and then finds leisure insupportable, one is caught up in a rather horrible paradox. Reading for such a person is "escapist" in a very special sense, and a very different sense from that in which mathematicians have escaped to numbers, philosophers to metaphysical speculation, historians to delving amid the remains of earlier ages—escaped from the clatter of dishwashing, the crying of children, and even the problem of how to pay the butcher. Escape from trivial reality into significant theory is one of the habits of civilized man. An even more interesting habit is escape from trivial reality into significant reality. Imaginative literature provides the most effective method for this latter kind of escape. But is this the function served by imaginative literature today?

That question is best answered by posing another. When the typical modern reader of novels "curls up with a book," with what attitude does he begin to read? Does he come to the book with an alert mind and an exercised imagination ready to meet the author halfway, to co-operate with him in making the escape world lively, illuminating, and provocative? Or is he completely passive, with mind and imagination numbed, expecting to be presented with a comfortable and soothing makeshift world, expecting the author to do all the work, expecting his own reactions to have been foreseen and catered to, so that his reading is not an activity but a sluggish acquiescence, a total surrender of intellectual and imaginative responsibility? It is when the latter is true—and it is true all too often—that reading becomes simply a drug. A book, however "great," offers only the *possibility* of stimulation, excitement, insight, illumination:

> We receive but what we give,
> And in our life alone does Nature live.

Aesthetic experience of any kind (as we shall try to show) is a two-way process: the reader must never surrender, but always co-operate. We may read a book to escape from trivial reality to significant fiction, but we must read *actively* if we wish to discover that significance. And we must develop, by conscious effort, the kind of imagination that can breed significance as the book impinges on the mind. Similarly, the typical visitor to a motion-picture theatre, sitting in cushioned darkness and passively awaiting the presentation of substitute experience, is in no state to appreciate any genuine example of the art of the screen even supposing that he should be presented with one. Too many books simply duplicate the atmosphere of the theatre, presenting the reader with a dark and cushioned seat where he can sit, comatose, comfortable, and undisturbed, and watch the standardized patterns of weakly imagined experience glide like fluent sedatives across the page.

Are the books or the readers to blame? Does this situation arise because people read books for the wrong reasons or because writers write the wrong sort of books? To answer this adequately would be to raise the whole question of mass education in a democracy. Mass education, as we have noted, too often means education at the lowest practicable level— the provision of minimum techniques with no concern about the ends which those techniques may serve. Perhaps readers only get the kind of books they deserve, and writers get the kind of readers they deserve. But it is useless to try to apportion blame: the important objective is to define the situation and to realize that it produces kinds of reading and kinds of writing that are complementary. What happens to literary value then?

Let it be said again that recreation, pleasure, even "escape" are not necessarily unworthy motives for reading. The question concerns the kind of recreation, the kind of pleasure, the kind of escape. Pleasures can be deadening or enlivening, profitless or fruitful, obscuring or illuminating. They can result in exciting and liberating rearrangements of existing patterns in the mind, or they can run only in existing grooves to confirm prejudices and exclude new insights. Factual books, works of science or pure history, writing whose object is simply to convey information, cannot have their purpose so easily corrupted: they can do neither as much good nor as much evil. But *corruptio optimi pessima,* and imaginative writing, which in our time almost always takes the form of prose fiction, can do great good or great harm.

In an age when reading is a passive rather than an active pleasure, or when it is not a pleasure at all (for it is doubtful whether pleasure is simply the absence of pain, and for most people reading fiction produces merely the absence of the irritating awareness of their own existence), few people would bother to justify seriously the writing of books about events which did not in fact occur. That such writing takes its place with the majority of motion pictures and radio programs in helping people to forget would be conceded. But critics today rarely pause to appraise the function of untrue stories in our culture. The serious critic will assume the significance of imaginative literature and, having assumed it, will feel free to discuss points of detail relating to special cases; and this is useful and often illuminating work, though it takes the answers to the fundamental questions for granted. Popular critics occasionally engage in well-meant but far too general discussion of great books and their meaning for all time. It might therefore be a useful approach simply to take a look at the books being written and read and ask, "Why read them?" A consideration of this question would naturally lead to the more fundamental questions of literary criticism and appreciation already indicated.

The situation is further complicated by the fact that "culture" still claims the respect even of those who have never paused to reflect on what it is or what it might be. A certain atmosphere of importance and even profundity has clung to the idea of literature in general, so that readers of every kind tend to have the feeling that in the mere act of reading books they are achieving some worthy end. Yet few readers today really believe with total conviction that reading fiction is a profound good; but it is comforting to think so, and to be reassured by the critics that it is so. One of the principal functions of book reviewers thus becomes one of reassurance: they must confirm readers in their somewhat vaguely held attitude that there is something intrinsically good about reading books. The reader does not demand from the reviewer any consistent set of principles—or, indeed, any principles at all. The reviewer may blithely confuse criticism with autobiography, fiction with journalism, poetry with philosophy or history. He may praise a novel one day because it reminds him of his childhood in a certain town; the following day he may praise another because it accurately diagnoses some general's failure in military strategy in the recent war; a third review may take the form of a simple summary of the plot of the novel under consideration; a fourth may hail a story because of the social evils it exposes or the political action it suggests; and a fifth novel may be welcomed because it is "well written" though otherwise of no particular interest. As long as reviewers of fiction can discuss novels as though they were really worth talking about, the content of their reviews means very little. Publishers support literary periodicals because they give countenance to the idea that literature is important. But a confused sense of the importance of literature does not make for literary discrimination or understanding, and universal awe before culture hinders rather than helps the critic.

Popular agreement that works of imaginative literature are somehow, in some vague and undefined sense, important blurs the edges of all the significant critical problems and encourages the cultural impostor. Aristotle's *Poetics* seems to have been in some degree a reply to Plato's condemnation of poetry as being an imitation of an imitation, and certainly Sir Philip Sidney's *Defence of Poesie,* with which

English literary criticism virtually begins, was written to counteract a fairly widespread distrust of works of the imagination. As Gregory Smith remarked in the introduction to his famous edition of Elizabethan critical essays, "Elizabethan criticism began in controversy": the attempt to discover and formulate the nature of literary value thus started, as far as English literature was concerned, as an attempt to defend literature, not to explain why everybody conceded its significance. Our civilization has inherited much both from Sidney and his opponents, with the result that Sidney's conclusions are more or less taken for granted while the point of view of the other side is nevertheless strongly represented in modern social behavior—witness the modern businessman's attitude toward the artist and the whole conflict between the artist and the "philistine," which has been with us for generations. If only the conflict were an open, intellectual conflict, as it was in Sidney's day, the understanding and appreciation of the arts might benefit; but so long as it exists against a background of apparent agreement that "art" and "writers" and "books" are in some sense valuable, it continues to confuse the issue. An open attack by representatives, say, of the modern business world on works of imaginative literature on the grounds that because they do not tell the truth they are useless or that they are harmful because they take up time that ought to be devoted to more "practical" activities would help to clear the air, and would precipitate a discussion in the course of which our modern confusion would be brought to light. But as things are we move in a flood of books, books which serve all sorts of purposes and which are praised for all sorts of reasons; and the critic who is concerned with the nature of literary value finds his enemies masquerading as his friends and the very object of his inquiry so manifold and confused that he hardly knows where to begin. Society assumes that people believe in both religion and art, though it does not like people to say so too loudly or too often. Both art and religion would be better off if their opponents were encouraged to speak out.

But if controversy on fundamentals helps to bring first principles to light and keep them in the light, one is not necessarily prevented from raising the more important questions by lack of overt disagreement about them. Having noted the difficulties in the way of a widespread understanding of what the real use and purpose of imaginative literature are, we may proceed to ask questions on our own account, ignoring, at least in the first stages of our investigation, both apparent agreement and real disagreement—both the popular belief in culture and the minor civil wars of the coteries—and raising the simple and basic questions with a deliberate innocence. Why, in fact, should we read books that tell of events which as a rule did not actually occur? If we start with this naïve query and follow, as Socrates did, "whithersoever the argument leads us," we may find ourselves eventually in a position to make all the distinctions and generalizations that we have already seen to be necessary. At least we shall be enabled to get behind the fog of equanimity to an area where things can be seen for what they are.

It should be added that the expression of this hope implies the nominalist rather than the realist answer to the old controversy. Works of literature *are* something, and it is possible to see them for what they are. And because they are something, they do something, they serve a certain purpose, have a certain use, in the light of which their value can be assessed. But what that purpose, that use, and that value may be can be discovered only at the end of our investigation. We do not wish to start by assuming any of the answers we are setting out to demonstrate.

‡ CHAPTER II ‡

The Literary Use of Language

THE HABIT of telling stories must have developed soon after man learned to speak. People have apparently always been interested in hearing the recital of a series of events irrespective of whether those events ever occurred or not. We need not delve deep into psychology in order to realize that curiosity concerning the possibilities of life is a deep-seated human characteristic. Interest in possibilities is more primitive and fundamental than interest in probabilities, and the inviting note of such an opening as "once upon a time" is a call to contemplate events not as symbols of man's fate but as examples of man's imagination. Whatever can be imagined can be imagined as happening or having happened, however far beyond our experience it might be. Events as such are interesting.

Naïve curiosity, wholly divorced from an interest in truth at any level, may thus account for the beginnings of storytelling. But curiosity alone will not keep a man interested in a story he has already heard. The desire to hear a story repeated means that it has done something more than satisfy a naïve curiosity. It has become exciting, or suggestive, or in some way worthy of attention after its original function has been served. It may be that the incidents narrated are of such a nature that they arouse ideas, and the listener finds these ideas worth dwelling on. The "plot" may have some kind of a "moral." If this accounts for the interest, then it is not likely that the listener will demand that the story be told in exactly the same words as before. But the interest may derive from other elements. It may be that the images used in telling the story in the first place were so vivid and memorable that they haunted the listener long after he lost interest in the events they were employed to describe—or they may, on the other hand, have given him a greater interest in the events. In either of these latter cases, his concern will be with the story as it was expressed in language when he first heard it, not with the events it narrated for what those events suggested as events. It must have been very early discovered (though perhaps not in a conscious way) that language is a means of expression that is not easily fitted in a neutral manner to a previously conceived content. The "content" takes on a new quality from the medium which communicates it.

Taletelling may well have begun in order to satisfy a simple kind of curiosity about possible situations, but it seems likely to have developed in an endeavor to recapture significance in tales already told. That significance may be bound up solely with the incidents narrated without any regard to the particular way in which the story was told: the point may be virtue rewarded, the weak prevailing against the strong (the story of David and Goliath combines both and, so long as it was told intelligibly, the point would emerge whatever particular set of words were used in the telling), or some such separable "moral." Or the significance may not be explicable in summary form at all, and may depend entirely, or very largely, on the fact that the story is told in *these* words in *this* order.

But your primitive storyteller, whether balladist or narrator of prose folk tale, is not interested in style as such: he is interested in style only insofar as it will make what he has to say more lively and memorable, and he knows that events, however improbable or even impossible, can only be made lively and memorable in narration if the language in which they are expressed, in addition to carrying the main line of the meaning, can simultaneously make vivid contact with experience as known to the most unadventurous. Perhaps the first requirement of narrative style is *empathy*—the ability to put the reader or listener into the midst of what is being described.

We have already suggested that interest in possibilities is more primitive and fundamental than interest in probabilities. When men first make up stories they are, presumably, fascinated by whatever is conceivable as a human fate. History is a much later, and in a sense a less fundamental, interest. Conceivable human fates suggest always the possibility that the laws of men and nature are not fixed in accordance with what we might deduce from our own experience, that possibilities of adventure are unlimited. At a later stage men find less satisfaction in contemplating possibilities which are merely conceivable but not probable. The laws of nature may not be what our own limited experience suggests they are, but the mind of man, which we know at first hand through introspection as well as from observation of our fellows, does suggest some characteristic patterns in which men work out their destiny. Let nature's laws be what they may—let fairies, dragons, phoenixes, do their best or worst—insofar as they act on man they are acting on what we know as well as on the subject in which we are most interested—ourselves. If primitive man ignores history as far too limited a field to be interesting, he does not for long ignore psychology, human nature. To be interested in human nature while remaining indifferent to the behavior of nonhuman factors is to set the stage for the development of literature out of mere narrative. We make man behave as we know him to behave from our own experience of ourselves and others; but we allow man to be acted on by whatever we can imagine. We can thus test every aspect of the mind, character, and emotions of man by bringing it into contact with anything at all. Fiction enables us to explore the recesses of man's head and heart with a torch; history allows us only the natural light of day, which does not as a rule shine into such places. Literature is man's exploration of man by artificial light, which is better than natural light because we can direct it where we want it. And a limited and tentative definition of "style" could be that use of language as a result of which we are compelled, while listening or reading, to see ourselves as the ultimate object of exploration—however fantastic the events narrated. The reader is projected into the midst of it all, not as observer or umpire (though he may be those as well) but as a fellow man. Curiosity about what may conceivably occur gives way to interest in man's fate, man's fate as man, as a doing and suffering creature whom we know because we are one ourselves.

History limits us not only to what has occurred, but to what we know to have occurred, which is only a tiny segment of man's behavior, and not necessarily that in which man is most recognizable. If we in fact could know every thought and action that men throughout the whole of history have ever thought and done, then Aristotle's dictum that poetry (by which he meant all imaginative literature) is "more philosophical and more serious" than history would not be true: for the facts would themselves supply such a rich treasury of true stories that we could construct significant arrangements of them without going beyond literal truth. To extend our earlier metaphor: if daylight could be directed at will to any place and to any time, we should not need artificial light.

Neither mere possibilities nor mere actualities are thus good enough for the storyteller who wishes his work to continue to arouse excited interest. That interest and that excitement derive from our continuous discovery of ourselves. In that sense, and in that sense only, does imaginative literature concern itself with "probabilities": a story *as told* must not do violence to man's fate as a doing and suffering being, known to us because of the fact that we are men ourselves. Men can, in literature, be possessed of all kinds of impossible and supernatural powers; they may live with an enchantress as Odysseus did with Circe or make pacts with the devil as did Faustus; but they must never escape their fate as men.

Do we, then, read works of imaginative literature simply in order to learn about ourselves? That must be at least part of the answer, though the adverb "simply" is misleading: that kind of self-knowledge is anything but simple. But imaginative literature is certainly a form of knowledge. It is, however, knowledge for no specific purpose, disinterested knowledge, knowledge which, uncorrupted by any immediate necessity to be put to some use, can be allowed to enrich our whole personality and make us more interesting and more interested as human beings. The phrase "art for art's sake" is meaningless in itself, for it implies no definition of art; but if we agree with the Aristotelian tradition to the extent of considering art a unique way of communicating a unique kind of knowledge, we can use the phrase at least in the sense that such knowledge is itself valuable and can be defended without reference to any further purpose it may serve. (And of course it may serve further purposes.)

II

At this point let us look a little more closely at the mechanics of narrative. A story is a record in language of a series of real or imaginary events; today we usually assume that in a novel the events are imaginary. As soon as events are described in language they take on quite new aspects and interests. To describe an event is in the first place to take it out of the welter of actual occurrences which jostle each other throughout time and of imaginary occurrences which may exist vaguely in the mind and to present it as something worth isolating. It is by implication invested with some kind of value. We may do our best to minimize that implication by describing the event in language that has as few overtones and suggestions as possible, but we can never altogether eliminate it. Once something is translated either from the world of actuality or that of mere imagination into some medium of communication—in this case, language—it takes on a quite different kind of life and value. To express something is to have that something in some way determined by the expression. John Smith is killed in New York: when we express that in language we are choosing from among the kinds of significance the event can have. If we use the verb "murdered" instead of "killed" there is immediately implied some interest in the person who killed Smith, the motive for the killing, and such kinds of meaning as those associated with the word "guilt." The area of suggestion will differ if we phrase the sentence actively ("Somebody killed John Smith") or passively ("John Smith was killed"). The contrast between the indefinite, potentially mysterious, "somebody" in the former example and the precise naming of the victim at the end of the same sentence raises all the possibilities associated with the beginning of a detective story. But in the latter example, we are at the end rather than at the beginning of a series of incidents, and the impulse is to go back into the life of this John Smith who was killed and inquire into its course, to trace the sequence that led to this fatal end. In the first case (to pick one out of numerous possible differences) an interest in Smith's assailant is suggested, while in the second the major interest is in Smith.

This simple example will indicate the enormous possibilities of verbal expression. If we take not a single event but a whole sequence of events, there seems to be no limit to the kinds of significance we can derive from them through the kinds of language in which we express them. Let us consider again the story of David and Goliath. Here is a situation which, as a situation and apart from the manner in which it is narrated, stands for a whole set of typical situations of a kind the human mind has always loved to contemplate—the despised but good little fellow getting the better of the bigger, stronger, but iniquitous giant. If, then, the situation itself can suggest significance, the possibilities of adding richer or subtler significance through the means of expression used in narrating it must be well-nigh infinite. It is this fact that makes literature possible as a permanent human activity.

All real events are part of history, and play their part as cause and as effect in the endless concatenation of human and natural behavior. Events as narrated by the skilled storyteller (whether true or not; the matter is irrelevant here) are, we might perhaps say, part of psychology. Their importance lies in how they are contemplated and where the receptive mind and emotions go from them. A good writer can, by his style, force whatever kind of contemplation he wishes on the reader. A good rhetorical writer can go so far as to induce action. The method of expression determines the reader's attitude. We can thus evaluate a work of literature by assessing the skill with which the expression is achieved, or by considering the significance of the attitude it is likely to arouse in the experienced and sensitive reader. (This distinction often becomes purely theoretical: in practice it may prove impossible to separate the two.) In fiction, we must also evaluate the fable, the pattern of action which, as we have seen, will in itself contribute (in varying degree) to the total significance of the work.

The difficulty of discussing a writer's skill in expression apart from the sense of significance that the expression communicates arises from the fact that the only way we have of testing the skill is to inquire what sort of significance the work cumulatively develops and communicates. Technique in literature is, in the last analysis, the means to an end, and can thus be truly evaluated only by a consideration of how effectively it produces a worth-while objective.

The craft of fiction demands in the first place what the

older critics called the proper "disposition of the fable."
That is, the pattern of events must be such that at every
point in the narrative the proper combination of retrospect
and anticipation is set up, the meaning of what has gone
before being continually enriched by what follows and the
meaning of what follows being continually enlarged by
what went before, and the meaning of the whole, because
of the way in which the action has been organized and arranged, emerging at the end as much more than the sum of
the parts. Elizabeth's acceptance of Darcy at the end of
Jane Austen's *Pride and Prejudice* has the significance it
does only because of the previous history of their relationship, of which her previous rejection of him is a most important part. And the meaning of both the earlier rejection
and the later acceptance is determined by the relation of
both not only to each other but also to all the other actions
of themselves and the other characters in the novel, the relation of heroine to hero being part of a pattern which is
the whole story, each part drawing enrichment from each
other part, so that the fact that Darcy and Elizabeth live in
the same world as Mrs. Bennet and Wickham must be seen
before the true meaning of each of them can be appreciated.
The significance of events in fiction is determined by the
world in which they are rooted. The writer of fiction must
therefore give us a world sufficiently simplified to enable us
to see everything in it as part of a single pattern and sufficiently complicated to allow us to see in each part, as well
as in the whole, reverberating meanings which linger in the
mind to produce ever deeper insights.

Life is a jungle of events whose meanings are at once too
casual (and to that extent insignificant) and too full of possible implication (without offering us any guidance as to

which implication or set of implications we should choose).
The skilled storyteller makes those meanings at once more
significant and less confused. He chooses or invents a trac-
table piece of life and proceeds both to define its meaning
more precisely than the meaning of any event in real life
can be known (Can we even talk of the "meaning" of events
in real life, unless we mean simply their causes and effects?)
and to enrich its meaning in a wholly unique manner. Is it
possible simultaneously to define a meaning more precisely
and to enrich it? We can see that this is possible if we consider what the skillful writer of fiction (and, indeed, of any
kind of creative literature) actually does.

Let us take a very simple example. Consider that a journalist has been asked to stand for a while in a city street
and then write up an account of the street and what took
place there. As soon as he begins to write he will have to
make his own definition of his subject. What in fact is meant
by "the street and what took place there"? To define even
the street requires a choice: is it simply the thoroughfare
leading from one place to another, or are we to include the
buildings which flank it, and if we include the buildings
what aspects of them are we to include? A street, in fact,
can be considered in an indefinite number of ways. As for
defining "what took place there," we strike here immediately the problem of selection. Clearly, it would be phys-
ically impossible as well as wholly pointless for the writer
to give an account of every single event which in fact occurred while he was there, or even of every single event
which he observed. Our journalist would have to select
from among the plethora of events—the actions and gestures
of people, the movement of traffic, all the innumerable
activities of city life—what he considered of importance or

of interest on some standard or other. He would have to define "street" and "what took place there" before writing or in the process of writing. And he would have to make up his mind about his perspective. Should he try to get closer to some things than to others; should he vary the distance at which he stood from people and things, or maintain a simple gradation from foreground to background? These and other questions he will have to answer, consciously or unconsciously, in presenting us with a verbal picture of that street at that time. Having done so, he will have presented to us aspects of a situation which we can recognize as one which we either have known or might have known. If he can use the language with any ability at all, even if he can put together a number of sentences which say, however badly or crudely, what he saw (or, rather, what he thought he saw) that he considered worth mentioning, we shall be able to recognize his account as corresponding to something of which we have had experience—assuming, of course, that we are products of the same civilization and are familiar with that kind of city street. That is to say, we should *recognize* the description as, in a general sort of way at least, true. The writer, without using any other skill than is required of a reasonably competent journalist, would have defined his subject intelligibly and recognizably. Out of the moving chaos of reality he will have isolated a static picture, which a certain class of readers would consent to, as reflecting in some sense an actual state of affairs.

Our journalist might do more than that. He might manage to convey to readers who have not had experience of that kind of city street at all a sense of the authenticity of his picture. He can do this by "style," by the selection and organization of his imagery, by using words in such a way that the reader is persuaded into recognizing not what he has seen but what he might have seen. The first stage is where we recognize what we know, the second is where we recognize what we might have known, and there is a third—where, while we recognize what we have known or might have known, we at the same time see, and know to be authentic, what we should never have seen for ourselves. The interesting fact is that where a writer succeeds in making authentic a picture of a kind that his readers might not have seen, he will very probably be doing more—he will be giving them at the same time a new insight which coexists with the feeling of recognition. This is because "style," that way of writing which makes convincing in its own right what would otherwise be merely recognizable, can rarely do this without going further. For such a style is the result of the ability to choose and order words in such a way that what is described becomes not merely something existing, something which happens to be in a particular place at a particular time, but something that is linked with man's wider fate, that suggests, and keeps on suggesting the more we read, ever wider categories of experience until there is included something with which we can make contact, which touches what we, too, find recognizable. And then it becomes irrelevant whether what is described exists in fact in the real world or not. The mere journalist drops his words one by one, and there they lie, in the order in which he dropped them, specific but still, corresponding accurately enough to what the author intends to say, but having no further life of their own. But the true creative writer drops his words into our mind like stones in a pool, and the ever-widening circles of meaning eventually ring round and encompass the store of our own experience. And—to continue the metaphor—in doing so they provide a new context for familiar things, and what has been lying half dead in our mind and imagination takes on new life in virtue of its new context, so that we not only recognize what we feel we knew but see the familiar take on rich and exciting new meanings.

If, therefore, the journalist who described what went on in a particular city street during a given period of time had the literary skill (and the initial combination of feeling for life and feeling for language which alone can make such a skill *realizable*) to present his observations in such a way that when he wrote of businessmen entering and leaving the bank, children coming home from school, housewives out shopping, loiterers, barking dogs, lumbering busses, or whatever else he cared to note, he was able to convey to the reader something of the tragedy or the comedy of human affairs, wringing some human insight out of these multifarious incidents so that the reader not only sees what he already knew or even admits as authentic what he did not know, but sees simultaneously what he knew and what he never saw before, recognizes the picture in the light of his deepest, half-intuitive knowledge of what man's experience is and can be and at the same time sees it as a new illumination—if he can do this, then he has moved from journalism into art. He has shown that he can make the means of expression comment on what is expressed so as simultaneously to define and expand his subject matter: define it by using words that block off the wrong meanings, which show with complete compulsion that what is meant is *this* rather than *that*, and expand it by choosing and arranging words and larger units of expression so that they set going the appropriate overtones and suggestions which help to elevate a description of people's behavior to an account of man's fate.

"Style" then—to employ this term for that use of language which distinguishes art from mere communication—is a handling óf words in such a way as to produce both recognition *and* insight. The experience of mere recognition is neither profound nor memorable, though it is the easiest to produce and appreciate. It is true that mere skill in communication or imitation can be by itself impressive: a writer who describes to us clearly what we know and a painter who produces a "good likeness" have achieved something of interest and value, but art is more than an *aide-mémoire* and we do not as a rule read novels to refresh our memory any more than we as a rule appreciate paintings because we are in love with the model. We may of course admire the sheer craftsmanship of a man who can draw a tree so that it looks exactly like a tree, but though this kind of skill produces agreeable and perhaps entertaining results, is it *in itself* more valuable than that of a man who, say, imitates perfectly the cries of birds? Is imitation of much value simply as imitation?

If by an adequate use of language we can make an account of *anything* rise from journalism to literature, where does the fiction writer come in, and what is the place of invention? Can any story, properly told, become significant literature? The fact is that writers seem to approach this matter of storytelling in one of two ways. They can take a plot of no particular interest from anywhere and derive continual and cumulative meaning out of it by the way they handle it. An obvious example of this method is Shakespeare's *Hamlet*. Shakespeare took an old story and gave it infinitely reverberating meanings by his disposition of the story, by the cause and effect relation which he breathed into the sequence of events, by the language in which at each point he enriched and vitalized and humanized the action. (For the purposes of the present discussion, fiction may be taken to mean any imaginative work which tells a story, whether in drama or in the novel.) The other approach is to invent or discover a story where the sequence of events in itself is suggestive and full of implication, and then write it in such a way as always to bring out the maximum of meaning. The Greek dramatists, for example, often seem to have done this. Feeling that the great myths of their people had vast symbolic meanings, they took the most suggestive of those myths and endeavored to bring out and reinforce the meanings by the poetic effectiveness of the style.

Style and plot are not, therefore, completely different means of achieving similar ends, with an author having the option of choosing either or both. Style—the way in which the action is handled at any given point, the selection and arrangement of words, images, sentences, paragraphs, and larger units so as simultaneously to define and enrich the action as it is unfolding—is plot seen through the microscope. Plot is the pattern of events, the relation of the parts to the whole and to each other, the rhythm of action in its broader aspects, the making of incidents symbolic by their interrelationships. Style is the continuous maintenance of the symbolic expansion of meaning through appropriate devices of language and arrangement. To choose a trivial example: it may make a difference in a novel of social satire whether a character is described as raising his hat or as uncovering his head. Insofar as this is a question of what aspect of the action to emphasize, it is a question of plot; but it is also a question of phrasing and thus of style. If we pursue the matter, we find style to be a function of plot: it is in fact the most effective treatment of plot at any given point.

If the function of style is to achieve a symbolic expansion of meaning, it is important to understand in what sense literature can be considered as symbolic expression. There are many kinds of symbols, and many definitions of the term, but as used here it simply means an expression which suggests more than it says. Perhaps everything expressed is in some sense symbolic, for individuals will always have their personal store of associations in the light of which even the most simple and literal statements may suggest more than they literally mean. But a novel is symbolic expression in the sense that the actions and characters described are interesting chiefly because of their ability to stand for *kinds* of actions and characters larger than themselves. This is not to say that a novel is merely a series of typical situations, though some are no more than that. A symbol is something in which sensitive men recognize their potential fate, tragic or comic or a mixture of both: that description of a city street, if done by a writer who is an "artist" as well as a journalist, will *implicate* the reader, whatever the extent of his personal experience of that kind of street, will produce in him a heightened awareness of the beauty or terror or mystery or some other aspect or group of aspects of human life. The writer will choose a method of expression which at each point will present the description as a description of more than what is being actually described, and this expansion of meaning will not be achieved by obvious appeals to the reader's emotions or by overt comparisons and allusions or by a diction disproportionate to the subject or by any of those facile devices which represent the offensive thrusting of the writer's intentions between the reader and the object; but subtly, delicately, so that the larger meanings emerge persuasively and cumulatively only after careful reading.

Subtlety in some degree is necessary because the reader must be allowed to read himself into the work as a result of what the work says, not of what the author deliberately does to him. The insights represented by art are never presented to the reader as insights, for that would be to destroy the fine mesh of narrative enticements by which the writer draws the reader into his imaginative world. Only when he is fully in that world will he be receptive to the values which it suggests. To talk about those values outside the texture of the novel is to separate what the book *is* from what it is *about*. The emotion must be in the book, not in the author. Of course it must have been in the author at some time, but Wordsworth's phrase "emotion recollected in tranquillity" is not a casual description of the origin of poetry; it applies to all art in that it makes clear that the aim of the artist is to construct a vehicle in which the emotion may live objectively, not one whose function is simply to relieve the artist's feelings.

In prose writing it generally takes time to achieve the proper effect: there must be a group of patterned incidents, rather than a single incident, for prose is a medium which, compared with poetry, achieves its effect expansively rather than intensively, depending less on sudden "explosions" of meaning in the reader's mind than on the progressive fusion of retrospect and anticipation in a more or less leisurely manner. To the prose writer time is a friend, for the parts are disposed in a temporal order and gather significance out of the way they succeed each other, while to the poet—the lyrical poet, at least, for there are other kinds of poetry to which this does not always apply—time is an enemy, for though he too arranges his words in an all-important sequence, past, present, and future elements in the expression must present themselves vividly and simultaneously to the mind if the true poetic effect is to be gained. The ideal reader of lyric poetry should have a perfect memory, since as a rule the poet is expressing in sequence (the sequence being made necessary by the nature of language) what was essentially to him an instantaneous though complex vision. A perfect memory is not, however, required of the ideal reader of prose, since the effect of prose writing is generally intended to be cumulative rather than instantaneous: when the reader reaches the climax of the narrative, if it is a narrative he is reading, it is proper that the climax should present itself most clearly to his mind, while all that led up to it, from the first sentence of the first chapter, disposes itself in his memory with varying degrees of distinctness, though nothing is actually forgotten.

Admitting, then, that prose expression is more likely to be effective as literature if it is of reasonable duration, we turn to prose fiction and realize that if it is to be the telling of a story whose events are so patterned and whose method of expression is at each point so artfully chosen that the sensitive and experienced reader will see in it more than the mere record of real or imaginary events, that he will rather discern continuously echoing new meanings which will persist in the mind and bring both conviction of old truth and suggestion of new, both recognition and insight—if it is to be this, it can only be so when the expression is continuously symbolic, continuously saying more than it means in the obvious, literal sense. The difference between journalism and literature (as between "scientific" and "artistic" writing) lies in the fact that the former is literal communication and the latter symbolic communication. This would be true, at least, where journalism is good journalism, the objective recording of facts of contemporary history: there are types of bad journalism which achieve neither literal nor symbolic communication but only a confusion of the two.

Language can thus be regarded as either a medium of communication or as a medium which can, while communicating, simultaneously expand the significance of the communication. The latter is the literary use of language and does not, of course, confine itself to prose fiction. (It should be said here that the terms "literary" and "artistic" are used in a similar sense: both refer to this kind of use of a medium of expression or communication, the former specifically to such a use of language and the latter more generally to such a use of any medium which can be used in that way. There are, of course, other and wider definitions of "literary," but at this stage in the discussion it will be most convenient to use the term to differentiate the kind of writing which produces a work of art from that which merely communicates.) The question arises whether the difference is one of kind or merely of degree. Does not any use of language set going meanings beyond the immediate literal meaning? In a sense, the difference would appear to be one of degree—though a large enough difference in degree becomes a difference in kind. It is largely a question of the writer's control over the potentialities of his medium. Casual impacts on individual sensibilities, which may be made possible only by the individual's unique state of mind, may achieve a literary effect on that individual. No writer can foresee that kind of random expansion of meaning, or the misunderstandings which often arise from the same cause. A college student discussing Milton's "Ode on the Morning of Christ's Nativity" in a classroom stated that he was given an impression of intolerable heat by the line

And bid the weltering waves their oozy channel keep.

It emerged in discussion that for him "weltering" suggested "sweltering," which accounted for his completely irrelevant and misleading impression of heat. Such a suggestion derived from purely personal factors, and his impression was not shared by any other reader. Similarly, just as random meanings may be picked out of lines or phrases in a work of literature, meanings may be accidentally put into them. (The phrase "I know that my redeemer liveth" in the book of Job has been understood for centuries by Christian readers in a sense never intended by the writer.) Even an occasional line in a work not literary in nature at all may, by a fortuitous juxtaposition of words, achieve a significance far removed from anything the author meant. But these exceptions only illuminate the fundamental rule: the artist always remains in control, and while he may not always be able to anticipate the effects of his work on different readers, he is organizing his expression in order to produce an effect greater than the mere communication of the literal meaning. The difference, then, between the literary and the non-literary use of language can be considered one of degree, resulting from a difference in the degree of control exercised by the writer.

The control may not be exercised by the writer with full awareness, but that it is exercised in some way becomes evident in every line of the work. Coleridge wrote "Kubla

Khan" automatically, in an opium daze, but he clearly exercised control over the progression of images. The nature of the control exercised by the artist is difficult to define—perhaps, insofar as it concerns the psychology of composition, it is a matter for the psychologist rather than for the literary critic—but the point is that, however he achieves this object, the artist does not allow the potentialities of his medium to manifest themselves aimlessly. The artist knows what he is doing, though he may not anticipate its effects: he knows that he is exploiting those potentialities of language which other writers release fitfully and by accident.

Can one isolate a phrase, a few lines, or a paragraph from a work of literature and discover from this fragment alone that it represents a literary rather than a nonliterary use of language? If the artist is concerned with the cumulative effect of his work, can we pass judgment until we have allowed the whole work to unfold itself? The answer to this question would seem to be that on the whole it is possible to recognize and to appreciate the literary use of language even in a part of the work, though full understanding and appreciation must, of course, await a full reading. Nevertheless, there are more cases where one cannot do this than are generally imagined. Keats's famous phrase in the final stanza of the "Ode on a Grecian Urn"—"Beauty is truth, truth beauty"—is not in isolation either poetic or exciting. In fact, by itself it is rather silly. We may think of it as poetic because we remember it in its context. Even if we quote both the final lines,

"Beauty is truth, truth beauty,"—that is all
Ye know on earth, and all ye need to know,

we cannot say that this is itself good poetry. Isolated in such a way, it sounds like an aphorism addressed to the reader rather than a final reconciliation of opposites phrased with reference not to the reader but to the figures on the urn. Mr. T. S. Eliot to the contrary, these two lines are clearly poetic, and poetically effective, in their context, at the conclusion of the poem; but by themselves they sound like a piously didactic paradox.

Different writers depend in different degrees on the time dimension. As a rule, as we have mentioned, lyrical poetry depends more than prose on its complete expression—and on an expression as simultaneous as the existence of the time dimension allows. But some poets do, in some degree, make the parts microcosms of the whole. And the extent to which a writer always has his eye on all the parts of the work may vary. Gray's "Elegy" is less tightly knit than the "Ode on a Grecian Urn." Paradox as it may seem, many of Donne's *Songs and Sonnets* ("The Canonization," for example) use the individual stanza as a microcosm of the whole to a greater extent than anything by Hopkins. The former example in each case can be more easily appreciated as poetry in its separate parts than the latter. In prose fiction, in spite of the fact that style is a function of plot, a single chapter may often convey something of the literary quality of the whole, though never its full significance. It is in non-fictional prose that the part may most often give the flavor of the whole. No more "microcosmic" writer exists than Sir Thomas Browne, whose prose is so richly harmonized that one could almost say that its meaning is conveyed vertically rather than horizontally. The whole theme of the *Religio Medici*, for example, is the paradoxical one that religion and irreligion really amount to the same thing: Browne is endeavoring to break down distinctions and include all things in a single context. Thus the very title tells his story: "the religion of a doctor" brings together the numinous and the scientific, all the more so because, as Browne points out at the beginning of his first paragraph, doctors are not generally considered religious. In sentence after sentence he reaches out to embrace apparent contradictions and bring them together; each sentence is thus a microcosm of the book as a whole—or, if this is pressing the point too far, it is certainly true of each paragraph.

We have reformed from them, not against them; for (omitting those Improperations and Terms of Scurrility betwixt us, which only difference our Affections, and not our Cause,) there is between us one common Name and Appellation, one Faith and necessary body of Principles common to us both; and therefore I am not scrupulous to converse and live with them, to enter their Churches in defect of ours, and either pray with them, or for them.

Here we have the whole of *Religio Medici* in little: reformation does not imply disagreement; any admission of difference is softly tucked away within brackets; and at the end there is the cunning suggestion that praying *for* somebody (which would really indicate that we are concerned for them because they are not of our faith) amounts to the same thing as praying *with* him (which indicates that we *are* of the same faith). The actual statement of the case—an appeal for toleration—is reinforced by stylistic devices and by every kind of pseudological suggestion that can be derived from language. One does not need to read the work through to see and appreciate what is going on. There is, indeed, a careful structure in the *Religio,* but it is significant that few readers have bothered to look for it: the prose is such that they do not need it. Browne almost achieves by depth alone what is generally achieved in more equal proportions by depth and expansion.

A similar writer, from this point of view, is James Joyce, who, though he patterns *Ulysses* with the greatest of care, so orchestrates each part that it almost tells the whole story. In fact, one of the problems with Joyce is that he is so careful to expand the meaning vertically at each stage that we cannot bring ourselves to bother much about the horizontal meaning. Of course, such vertical expansion does not mean that literary expression can ever take place in an instant. In music, complex orchestration does not eliminate horizontal structure, communication over a period of time; and there is no reason why it should do so in literature. But it might be argued that language, being a medium that has meaning independently of the form into which it is arranged, stands less in need of both chords and melody—or at least that if you complicate the line of meaning by using sentences (as it were) as chords, you cannot project the line of meaning too far without asking the reader to carry too difficult a burden. Joyce in *Finnegans Wake* goes so far as to use individual words as chords, making them carry an echoing meaning far beyond what can be carried by a musical chord. A musical chord in isolation can perhaps suggest finality, or triumph, or some simple and definite emotion, but a verbal chord, made up of parts of different words welded together in a complex pun, can provide a wealth of specific meaning simply by the simultaneous suggestion of those different words. Even in *Ulysses,* with such a comparatively simple verbal chord as "Lawn Tennyson," Joyce was able to convey a sense of Tennyson's connection with the stately homes of England and of the whole modern attitude to Victorian England without putting these two words into a sentence at all. Literary writing is always writing on different levels simultaneously—on the literal and the symbolic, to put the matter at its most general—but the main burden is carried by extension, not by depth. Joyce tried to equalize the burden, which is perhaps to attempt the impossible. For the richer your chords the less you are in need of plot, yet the more complicated you feel impelled to make the plot. One great verbal chord which said everything simultaneously and made horizontal expansion unnecessary was perhaps Joyce's real ideal, but in striving toward it he got more and more involved in structure, for he tried to fill out the deficiencies of the chords by making them contribute to a melodic line. This is natural in music, but when carried too far in literature it becomes a self-frustrating device.

The literary equivalent of the melodic line need not be narrative: it can be speculation, rhapsody, description, discourse of any kind. Narrative is, however, one of the most effective ways of developing and communicating literary insight. The construction of a plot, in the more ordinary sense of the phrase, will not only help the reader to follow the cumulative meaning of the whole, but provides a skeletal fable from which the subtler implications can develop. In nonnarrative literature the burden falls more heavily on the technique of expression as such. In great dramatic poetry such as Shakespeare's we have all the advantages of the skeletal fable with a rich exploitation of technical resources generally employed by other writers only when there is no fable to help along the meaning—which is what makes Shakespeare's plays so overwhelming in their significance. Narrative, however, and the less rich, less lyrical techniques appropriate to prose narrative, have become the norm of modern literature. The novel has long been the most popular literary form, and for that reason if for no other the aesthetics of the novel requires more detailed consideration.

CHAPTER III

The Nature of Fiction

THE STORY of David and Goliath has already been cited as a "symbolic" story: it symbolizes the victory of the weak over the strong, and at the same time that of good over evil, and in doing so satisfies the primitive human desire to see bullies thrashed and evil men done away with. The symbolism here is at a quite elementary level, and it derives from the nature of the action irrespective of how that action is expressed in words. Exactly the same point would be made if we saw the story told in a series of pictures. A simple symbolic situation of this kind does not depend on the resources of any medium of communication: it is self-contained and explicit.

The pleasure we get out of hearing or reading such a story is, presumably, that of wish fulfillment. This is an account of something we should all like to see done, and it stands for the kind of thing we should like to see done at all sorts of levels. Are we justified in calling this kind of pleasure a "literary" satisfaction? Is it one of the pleasures of art? Many of the Renaissance critics would probably have answered in the affirmative. Poetry, argued Sir Philip Sidney at the end of the sixteenth century, is a more effective teacher than history because it shows us good men getting their reward and the wicked receiving their just deserts. Imaginative writing, he thus infers, is justified because it incites to virtue by appropriate examples. "If evil men come to the stage, they ever go out so manacled as they little animate folks to follow them. But the historian, being captived to the truth of a foolish world, is many times a terror from well doing, and an encouragement to unbridled wickedness." The pleasure in seeing poetic justice done, Sidney would have argued, following a line of thought common in his age, is characteristic of imaginative literature rather than of history and philosophy; and it is a wholly justifiable pleasure because it is moral in its end—it leads us to pursue virtue and shun vice.

So long, therefore, as such wish-fulfilling stories fulfill *moral* wishes, such as the desire to see good flourish and the wicked destroyed, the pleasure aroused by these stories would be, in a sense, a moral pleasure and thus a justifiable one to those who hold, as Sidney did, that the ultimate function of art is didactic—to "teach delightfully." "Poets wish either to instruct, or to delight, or to combine the two," wrote Horace some sixteen hundred years before Sidney. The doctrine is not unusual. Suppose, however, that we take satisfaction in a story which fulfills an immoral wish? There can be no question that people do take delight in such stories. There are many things most people would like to do but are restrained from doing by the law or by public opinion, and a story, however crude or simple, will often appeal because it provides a substitute fulfillment of those immoral desires. Wish fulfillment as an objective of fiction is thus independent of didacticism, so that even if we agree with Sidney we are not necessarily committed to a belief in the value of wish fulfillment as achieved by literature.

All stories are not as simple as that of David and Goliath, but its simple symbolic nature, and the clearly understandable reaction it produces, illustrate a quality common to much fiction and a response found among many readers. The question of whether wish fulfillment is (a) a legitimate literary function and (b) a valuable function remains the same whether we are discussing David and Goliath or the latest erotic best seller. Both stories depend for their effect on the actions described rather than on the literary skill with which they are described; both are symbols of what we should like to do or see done. The answer to the second part of this question is not difficult to find. Wish fulfillment in this sense may have a therapeutic value for the individual; the moral or other satisfaction given him by contemplating the action narrated may do him some good psychologically—or it may not. It would depend on the individual case. In the case of the erotic best seller, the substitute wish fulfillment is more likely to be psychologically harmful, because there are some wishes that it is frustrating to have fulfilled by substitution. But this is a matter for the psychologists to wrangle over. For our present purpose it is clear that wish fulfillment in itself is not necessarily a good reason for reading a book, though if it is combined with persuasive moral examples it may have a useful didactic function.

The first part of our question— Is wish fulfillment a "legitimate" literary response?—depends really on all the other questions we can ask about the nature of literary value, many of which will be raised in the succeeding pages. But this at least we can say at this stage: insofar as this kind of reaction depends entirely on what happens in the story and not in the least on the way in which the medium of language is used, it cannot be a reaction which depends on those aspects of language which distinguish art from journalism or simple history from great fiction. To this extent it cannot be a "legitimate" literary response; it does not arise from the characteristic differentiating qualities of literature.

The simple invention of a sequence of events is not necessarily a literary activity; literature can only arise when an attempt is made to communicate that sequence of events. Plot in itself is at best only potential literature. This view is not altogether inconsistent with Aristotle's statement that "plot is the first principle and as it were the soul of tragedy," for plot in this sense is the raw material of incidents out of which literature *may* be created; it does not become even potential literature until it has been carefully patterned, until the events have been invested with some kind of causation and inevitability. Plot is the "soul" of tragedy in the sense that it is essential, not that it is sufficient. The symbolic quality that arises simply from the sequence of events as a sequence is not in itself good enough for literature. There are several reasons for this. Events in themselves may be symbolic, but symbolic only of what we already know or expect. What happens to human beings is of course always of some kind of interest to us as fellow human beings; but unless the events are presented in such a way that insight is developed out of interest, the interest can only be a passing one. It is only the adequate literary treatment of a sequence of events which can give it that continuously expanding and reverberating symbolic significance which distinguishes great fiction from mere fable. Further, it could be argued that the value of fable, when it is a purely moral value, is not in itself a literary value at all, though it is not incompatible with literary value.

All imaginative literature is the symbolic expression of aspects of the human situation, and the difference between the various kinds of imaginative literature (for example, between lyric poetry and prose fiction) stems in some degree from the difference in devices employed to achieve this end. Symbolization is the artist's business, and there are many ways of effecting it. What distinguishes symbolization in art from other kinds of symbolization is largely the constantly expanding and reverberating meaning of the symbol. We may make x symbolize a number or a relationship in algebra, or a laughing cow symbolize a brand of milk. Our world is full of such nonliterary symbols. They may be simple symbols of what is complicated, concrete symbols of what is abstract, known symbols of what is unknown, constant symbols of what is variable; they may be badges, formulas, slogans, trade-marks—any of a thousand different things. They are all *more convenient* ways of referring to something else; they are not, as literary symbolization is, ways of expression which in themselves increase the significance of what is expressed in such a way that the means of expression alone provide continually expanding new insights into what is expressed to the point where it becomes impossible to distinguish the method of expression from what is said, the form from the content.

The great writer of fiction does not take a story and dress it up in "literary" language. His imagination may be first set to work by some existing story, as Shakespeare's so often was, but he does not proceed simply to "write up" that story as a journalist writes up a fire. The situations which the artist takes from tradition are cast into the fiery furnace of his creative imagination where they take on that unique and exciting form which *is* the new story, not simply its dress. What the characters do and are and what happens to them can from now on be adequately told only in the words of the artist who has forged the new story. A work of literature means what it says, and means all that it says: it never means what someone else can say that it says. The true meaning includes all the suggestions and cumulative insights which derive from adequate symbolization, adequate enrichment of meaning at all points through style, pattern, plot, rhythm, tone—*everything*. Ideally, there is no such thing as the subject of a good novel. There is only the novel.

One can see this even in a well-told adventure story. If one summarizes the plot of Stevenson's *Treasure Island,* one will not convey the slightest impression of the meaning of the book as it actually emerges to the reader. From a summary, for example, one would gather that the important thing in the novel was to obtain the treasure. As we read the book, however, we realize that the nearer we get to the treasure the less important it becomes—in fact, when it is finally obtained it is dismissed in a sentence: "All of us had an ample share of the treasure, and used it wisely or foolishly, according to our natures." The search for the treasure—an example of the age-old device of the quest—is but a part of a pattern of incident and characterization which, expressed as Stevenson expressed it, builds up in the reader as he reads that whole sense of picturesque danger, of colorful evil and purposeful virtue, of mystery as an essential flavor of life, of contrast between the familiar and the remote, the routine and the unexpected, the known and the unknown, which combine to symbolize persuasively and irresistibly that whole tract of human experience which can be labeled "love of adventure." The book is not about a hunt for treasure: it is about Treasure Island, and Treasure Island is itself a potent symbol, standing for the quest, and for a special kind of quest, the boy's quest, with all the implied further symbols of pirates, hidden maps, and southern seas. A world of geography, of psychology, of history is contained in the very title, which is an organic part of the novel and sets going right at the beginning the overtones which give added richness to—and are enriched by—the story itself as it unfolds. The symbolization has begun with the very title. What the title really says can only be told in the story itself as Stevenson wrote it. The critic can only poke about on the outside, picking out pieces which have no real life except in the context which the author provided for them. A novel is what the author says, not what the critic says. It is a commonplace that if a mere critic can present by summary and description the full meaning and significance of a work of literature, then it cannot be really a work of literature. Good books can be talked about infinitely—that is one kind of literary value, the capacity to provoke other people's insights—but they can never be adequately summarized or described.

If we can talk this way about such a comparatively simple work as *Treasure Island,* in which the symbolization is deliberately restricted to the demands of a juvenile imagination, it is clear that in works of greater stature the richness of implication is far more impressive and the possibility of adequate summarization correspondingly more remote. At this stage, indeed, the critic is tempted to lay down his pen. Why write books about books? Great literature is meant to be read, and the more we read the more we understand the nature of literary value. And yet it is not so simple as that. In an age when the production of books has become a major industry, when a continuous and bewildering stream of new works continually falls from the press, when fiction has become the standard disguise assumed by every kind of writing—historical, journalistic, rhetorical, diagnostic, biographical, philosophical, to mention only a few—it becomes important to inquire into the distinguishing features of imaginative literature and to investigate its characteristic function. The fact alone that people read books for so many different reasons raises the question of whether there is a "right" reason for reading some particular kind of book. When any activity is taken for granted it is useful to investigate its real nature and value.

The writer of fiction creates insights through his means of expressing a series of imaginary situations. Once we see that, we see more clearly what we are reading when we read a novel; we know what to look for and we know when (and if) we have found it. The kind of insights provided by imaginative literature are unique, because they are not communicated directly but through the symbolization of events, characters, and all the other elements in a story. That symbolization is achieved by the means of expression, and the insights it produces are accompanied by *recognition*. We both recognize what we know to be true and see what we did not know before. Now one can communicate new insights through philosophy and recognizable situations through journalism: philosophy, that is to say, communicates insight without recognition, and journalism communicates recognition without insight. Only imaginative literature communicates both simultaneously. Too many readers of novels, concerned only with the insight or with the recognition, approach fiction either as journalism or as philosophy and thus never succeed in obtaining any idea of the value of a novel as fiction, as the kind of literature whose glory is to be able to convey unique insights *through* the way it conveys a recognizable human situation. The academic critics who write or lecture on the ideas of Fielding or Thackeray and then separately discuss their "technique," thus inculcating the false gospel that a novel can be looked at *either* as a work of philosophy *or* as a piece of craftsmanship and that the way to appreciate it is to look at it first in one capacity and then in the other, help to confuse the issue. In literature the whole is never the sum of the parts.

The discussion up to this point has enabled us to frame some sort of a definition of fiction which might go somewhat as follows: Fiction as an art form is the narration of a series of situations that are so related to each other that a significant unity of meaning is achieved; the situations are presented in language such that at each point in the progress of the narrative the kind of relation between retrospect and anticipation is set up that continually and cumulatively reinforces the desired implications of the plot, so that the plot becomes symbolic as well as literal in its meaning. One definition of a "bad novel" would therefore be a novel in which no adequate complex of meaning has been achieved, where the devices of style, structure, etc., which the author has employed have not been adequate to shape the work into an illuminating unity. The reasons for the author's inadequacy would of course vary. He may have lacked that primary requisite of the novelist, the ability to hold his subject as a luminous whole in his mind as he writes. (For though it is possible to write a good novel episodically, without knowing the ending until you have almost arrived at it, you must hold the pattern richly in the mind within each episode: but this is a point we must investigate later.) He may simply have had no compelling vision to guide him in arranging or expressing his material. Or he may have had such a vision but lacked the familiarity with his medium—language—to express it adequately. If it was the latter defect, we may say that his vision might have been an impressive one, but it cannot have been a literary one—it cannot have been the kind of insight which, so far as it is communicable, depends on and even in a sense derives from the form and manner of expression. In general, the unsuccessful novelist lacks, for one reason or another, the ability to place the resources of his medium fully at the disposal of his *intention*. In the mature artist the intention itself will have been formed with reference to what expression in language can achieve. (A character, for example, would be conceived not simply in psychological terms, but in terms of a pattern of appropriate action and of the way such action would be expressed in words.)

Theoretically, there should be no such thing as a good novel ill written. For the goodness of a novel does not consist in the bright ideas or psychological knowledge or skill in contriving "situations" which the author may possess. These are not in themselves literary virtues: they are virtues of the philosopher, the psychologist, or the showman. A novel is good only if the whole pattern of expression (and this would include both style and plot) is adequate to achieve, continuously and cumulatively, that symbolization of event and character which alone distinguishes literature from journalism. Implication, enrichment of meaning, reverberating significances, are achieved by the artist through the way he handles his medium, in such a way that *what* he says and *how* he says it are indistinguishable. To say that a novelist "writes well" is to say that he has managed to achieve this, and, conversely, if he has not achieved it he cannot have written well. The phrase "writes well" seems to distinguish between what is written and what is written *about,* and this is a false distinction in imaginative literature. This whole way of discussing fiction is therefore misleading. "A good novel but badly written" is a defensible phrase only if we interpret "good" and "badly written" in very special senses; usually it is employed to mean that the critic likes the ideas expressed by the novelist (that is, he is judging the novel as philosophy or a contribution to some specific branch of knowledge) and is able to discern those ideas even though they are not well expressed. "A bad novel but well written" generally means that the critic is judging the quality of the writing on some other standard than that required by the novel. He might mean that he dislikes the ideas in the novel (again, judging it as a work of philosophy or science) but concedes that they are clearly and effectively expressed. He might even mean that what he is judging is not really a novel at all, but a series of sketches disguised as a novel, and that, considered as a series of sketches (or some other nonfictional literary form) it is well done. It is possible to see in a bad novel qualities of writing that would stand a man in good stead if he were writing history or journalism or advertisements. It is possible for a man to handle language in a craftsmanlike manner yet have serious imaginative defects. It is conceivable that one might say of a bad golfer that he swings his club nicely, but obviously he could not really be said to swing his club nicely from the point of view of golf or he would not be a bad golfer: the observer must have been applying a quite different standard, perhaps an aesthetic one, meaning that the actual movement was pleasing to the eye. That makes about as much sense as saying that as a golfer, a man was a good ballet dancer. And there *is* a certain amount of sense in such a statement, paradoxical though it is. A bad novelist who writes well must therefore be a writer from whose way of writing novels one infers that he might possibly be able to do some other kind of writing with success. He has certain skills, one might mean, but they are not adequate or not appropriate here.

The trouble arises from the fact that to judge fiction as fiction is very difficult, while to judge it as history, sociology, or rhetoric is fairly easy. We all tend to take the line of least resistance and judge a piece of writing on the standards that are most easily applied. The matter is further complicated when, as so often happens, works are presented as novels which are not in fact intended to be novels at all. The most complicating factor of all lies in the fact that a good novel can also be good on some other standard and can thus be judged in one of two ways. It would be easier if there were always a clear-cut line between, say, art and propaganda. But there is not. Most of the great nineteenth-century novels were written as propaganda—not perhaps primarily so, but certainly incidentally so. It is easy enough to see that *Uncle Tom's Cabin* is a piece of propaganda and ought to be judged as rhetoric (for fiction can be rhetoric), but what about the propaganda elements in Dickens? Dickens, though he has some obvious faults, is a very considerable novelist, and we read him today as a novelist, not as a propagandist. In his own day, however, he was both.

We can see this problem more clearly if we see that a writer can have two purposes, a general and a specific, which need not be incompatible so long as the latter can be included in the former. A satirist could be attacking some particular individual and at the same time some aspect of human frailty in general, so that whether one read the work as a personal attack or a general satire would depend on whether one happened to know the person attacked and also that the writer was in fact attacking him. Shakespeare's *Richard II*, played on the eve of a rebellion by supporters of the Earl of Essex, was taken as an attack on Queen Elizabeth—and it was so intended by those who arranged that particular performance. Professor Dover Wilson thinks that Hamlet may have been intended by Shakespeare as a portrayal of that same Earl of Essex. These intentions, by actors or author, were, however, perfectly compatible with the larger meanings of the two plays: Hamlet might have been Essex to a few initiated, but he has a much larger meaning to the world in general. The important question is: If a work has two objectives, can they be achieved by the same technique, and can the larger subsume the lesser?

The fact is that a work of art can serve a great number of different functions provided that each function is progressively wider, and the true aesthetic function can profit by the techniques demanded by the minor functions. Fiction— to embark on yet another definition—is the narration of real or imaginary events in which the incidents and characters are arranged in such a pattern, both in relation to each other and to the work as a whole, and in which the method of expression at any given point is such, that the resultant work is at the same time recognizable and convincing as a report on aspects of the human situation and illuminating as a series of original insights into human experience. But is it possible, in arranging this pattern, to make it at the same time serve the purpose of illuminating (and so by implication attacking) a specific contemporary abuse or of making some other kind of point which has meaning only with reference to a particular set of circumstances? The history of literature clearly shows that it is in fact possible, under certain conditions. *Gulliver's Travels* is a satirical picture of mankind as well as an indirect picture of Swift's own age and the particular aspects of his own society which most annoyed him. One can build a battleship in order to hunt down a fishing boat, but your battleship, once built, is also capable of much larger functions.

Very often, however, the devices required for the immediate purpose are encumbrances from the larger point of view. It is possible for art to be both good art and good propaganda, but it is also possible for the propaganda elements to corrupt the art. The propaganda purpose can result in a distortion of scale, a wrenching of the pattern, a crack in that mysterious welding of the parts to each other and to the whole which is the very essence of creative activity. Some of Dickens' novels would be better if he had not overemphasized certain elements at the expense of the total pattern. It requires a particularly cunning artist to make sure that the devices employed to secure the smaller purpose take their place naturally and effectively among the devices which achieve the larger. A rhetorical pattern— to put the same point in more strictly literary terms—is not incompatible with an aesthetic pattern, though few writers have the skill to fuse the two completely. The rhetorical purpose of Dickens no longer interests us; we read him for the aesthetic patern; and because there are in his novels devices which are not necessary for the completion of the aesthetic pattern (but which were necessary for those who read the book as rhetoric) we often recognize a certain looseness of structure.

A rhetorical and an aesthetic intention are not, then, contradictory, but the most effective rhetoric is likely to be "nonaesthetic" and the best art is likely to be non-rhetorical, if only because rhetorical art must employ devices which, on a purely aesthetic standard, are either unnecessary or confusing. *Uncle Tom's Cabin* was better rhetoric in its day than anything Dickens ever wrote, if by good rhetoric we mean rhetoric that influences the most people to the most direct action.

But the phrase "in its day" gives away an important difference between art and rhetoric. The former employs devices which, by and large, are equally effective at one time and at another, whereas the latter employs devices whose effectiveness may weaken or altogether disappear with the lapse of time. We may analyze the structure of the speeches of Demosthenes, but they do not influence us, and therefore for us they are not rhetoric but exercises in rhetorical method. But the plays of Sophocles are still art. Further, Demosthenes as a rhetorician was less effective than Hitler—which means that good rhetoric (again, in the pragmatic sense of rhetoric which influences most people) is to be distinguished from a great speech. (It might be claimed with some reason that a great speech is a speech which would have the most influence on an ideally educated audience. Until all audiences are ideally educated, the distinction between good rhetoric and a great speech will remain.)

The man who tries to combine rhetoric with fiction is writing for two audiences at once—one interested in the immediate (and smaller) issue and another interested in the less immediate and larger. If, therefore, the author can present his incidents in such a way that they are adequately symbolic on both levels—on the aesthetic and the rhetorical —he has solved the problem of combining these two modes of writing. Few fiction writers have achieved this. Dickens rarely managed it, with the result that some of his rhetorical devices are found intrusive by modern readers. Most modern novelists try to achieve this combination, which perhaps is some excuse for the critics who show confusion in applying standards to contemporary fiction.

The matter is further complicated by the fact that modern novelists often try to put across their meaning both through the relation of the events they describe to the events of real life today *and* through the pattern as a whole. They thus produce a species of art which claims some of the qualities of history and which is therefore open to both historical and aesthetic appraisal. This would give us another possible meaning for the phrase "a bad novel but well written." It might mean that the work is true as history but not presented in such a manner as to raise it from history to fiction. Steinbeck's *Grapes of Wrath* could be assessed either on a historical standard (what is the relation of what he writes to the actual problems of migratory workers?) or on a literary one (how illuminating a picture of the human situation does he present?). As a matter of fact, *The Grapes of Wrath* could be conceived as having three functions—rhetorical, historical, and literary (or aesthetic). Steinbeck almost succeeded in combining the first and the last of these by the simple and effective device of drawing his characters somewhat over life size, so that even the reader interested only in the rhetorical aspect had to stand back to the proper "aesthetic distance" in order to see the work—and in doing so he was forced to read it as art rather than as rhetoric or history.

This question of "aesthetic distance" is important. The term may be pedantic but the idea behind it is fairly simple. Every work of literary art, by its diction as well as other devices, provides an implicit set of directions concerning the distance from the object at which the reader must stand if he is to see it for what it is. Other arts have similar devices for indicating distance. This is most easily seen in poetry, where the difference between Pope and Wordsworth, or between Milton and Burns, is essentially a difference in the aesthetic distance required by the works of each. The more elevated the theme the greater the distance, and technical devices (e.g., diction) must be so arranged that they keep the reader at that distance. (The reason why so few English-speaking readers appreciate Racine or Corneille is that they underestimate the aesthetic distance required for the proper reading of these writers.) Now Steinbeck endeavors to set a certain distance between himself and his readers which will enable his novels to be read as novels rather than simply as propaganda; but at the same time his intense feeling for the contemporary problems involved leads him to narrow that distance. In *The Moon Is Down,* for example, the author, in his capacity as an interpreter of a universal theme (a variant, it might be noted, of the David and Goliath theme), employs a type of symbolic incident which requires a comparatively remote aesthetic distance for its proper appreciation. But Steinbeck as a rhetorician intent on persuading his readers that all was not lost even though countries like Norway were for a time under Nazi occupation required a much less aesthetic distance: he needed incidents that were less symbols in the aesthetic sense than *examples* of what was happening in Europe. It was this confusion between incident as symbol and incident as example that so bewildered the critics and drove them into two camps.

It is possible to read *The Moon Is Down* at the aesthetic distance required by the work as a work of art purely, and as such it has a certain quiet dignity and effectiveness, but it is too thin to be an adequate interpretation of the more universal aspects of its theme. It is too thin because so many of the incidents can barely stand the strain of expansion from example of contemporary events into symbol of a universal situation. It was stated at the time the book was published that the author was presenting "the theme that a free brave people is unconquerable." In the simple historical sense this statement is, unfortunately, not true. Yet it could be made to be true in a certain sense. For there is perhaps a sense in which the free and the brave are unconquerable (a sense hinted at in Aeschylus' *Prometheus Bound*). But it is not the historical sense, and in confusing symbol with example, fiction with history, aesthetic probability with contemporary actuality, Steinbeck made it difficult if not impossible for his readers to see in what sense he was treating his theme.

To achieve symbolization of events and characters in fiction is not the same as to make examples of them. An example is simply a sample case, a typical instance, while the symbolic expression we find in good fiction is an expansion of meaning that produces new insight into the nature of the whole. An example is a short way of letting us know what a lot of things are, and if we had time to look at all the things we would not need the example. A symbol, in the sense intended here, is not simply a timesaver; it tells us very much more than we could possibly discover by looking over all possible events as they actually occurred in history. A symbol both illuminates and comments on what it stands for, while an example simply indicates that a lot of other things are just like itself. Science uses examples, but art uses symbols.

Too many modern novels set out simply to give examples of how people behave under certain conditions or in certain parts of the world. They are psychological or geographical examples. As such they may be contributions to knowledge, but they do not communicate that unique kind of knowledge which it is the function of imaginative literature to communicate. In the last analysis, all literature is a contribution to knowledge of one kind or another; but that symbolization of expression which produces in the reader simultaneous insight and recognition gives a kind of knowledge that cannot be translated into any other terms. And it is not only a question of providing insights: imaginative literature—poetry, fiction, drama—provides a heightening of our self-consciousness as human beings which is itself pleasurable. It is pleasurable largely for the paradoxical reason that it is impersonal. To have one's awareness of one's own self-consciousness as a human being increased without any autobiographical emotions being directly involved is an achievement possible only to art.

But let us look more closely at this idea of the symbol in fiction. The reverberating meanings which actions and characters considered as symbols set up may start from many different points. We may have, for example, the historical symbol, where the characters and actions are presented in such a way as to illuminate attitudes and ways of living which are associated particularly with a given time. Or we may have the geographical symbol, as in the regional novel, where the attitudes and ways of living which are illuminated are associated with a given place. But whether we start off with time or place, we cannot, if we are writing a novel which is to be remembered as a work of imaginative literature rather than as a work of history or science, be content with expanding the meaning in a purely historical or geographical sense. In a historical novel the historical symbols must also be symbols of the human situation: the story must illuminate not only an aspect of man's past but also an aspect of man's fate. And the same is true of the geographical or any other kind of symbol. We may start off with the immediate intention of giving the reader new insight into a certain time, or place, or class, or point of view, or type of conflict—our symbols may be historical, geographical, sociological, philosophical—but that kind of symbolization, in an adequate novel, is only the thin end of the wedge, as it were, for the meanings echo and expand until the limited intention is wholly transcended, and Jeanie Deans in Scott's *Heart of Midlothian* is no longer an example of a lower-class Scottish girl of the eighteenth century but a symbol of a human situation which the reader recognizes both as true and as new, as confirmed by his own experience and as revealing what lies beyond it. In short, one might say that the historical novel which is *only* a historical novel is not in the full sense a novel.

This is important, because critics are often fooled by the mere picturesqueness of bygone manners into imagining that a lively account of them in an invented or part-invented story itself constitutes a good historical novel. But the depiction to one age of what appears picturesque in another can never in itself make a good novel, if only because picturesqueness is a purely relative quality, brought into existence by distance in time or space. Whether something is picturesque or not depends on the position in time and space from which we happen to be looking at it. Scottish fishwives are picturesque to English tourists, who like to think of them as such, just as western cowboys are picturesque to New Yorkers. This is a quality which, like "quaintness," depends on the extent to which we are prepared to kid ourselves. Scottish fishwives are not picturesque to each other or to members of the community in which they live, any more than cowboys are picturesque to other working cowboys. To depict an age or a region in such terms is to give a wholly artificial meaning to the life described; it is to describe what is distant in time or place in terms of its difference from ourselves rather than in terms of man's universal destiny. Such activity can be an interesting or amusing stimulant to a jaded mind, and it has its place among the minor kinds of writing. But it can never be either good history (for one can never hope to understand the past by treating it simply as quaint) or good literary art (since the literary artist can never operate by *exclusion,* by dwelling on what differentiates the generations from each other, but seeks to set in motion infinitely echoing meanings which combine and interact so as to present man's behavior as man's fate).

The symbolic meaning of characters and incidents in fiction can, as we have seen, *begin* by being merely historical, geographical, or some other kind of symbols, but that is simply the thin end of the wedge, the device for capturing the attention of the reader in the first place. Once that is done, the meanings broaden out and the historical, geographical, or other illustration becomes a comment on that aspect of man's fate to which it is most effectively related. Thus we might write a novel set in late fourteenth-century Europe in which the decadent splendor of a dying age of chivalry could be presented as a comment on and illumination of all that desperate pageantry with which man has from time immemorial tried to cover up his failures. Not that such a comment would be made explicitly or deliberately: it would emerge from the way the tale was told.

From all the foregoing it will have become apparent that a novel, insofar as it is an example of the "creative imagination" and a literary art form, has a kind of integration of meaning which the critic who tries to isolate its "message" or its style prevents himself from seeing. The fact is that the criticism of fiction is still at a very elementary stage. In discussing poetry we have got beyond the stage of investigating whether it presents elevating sentiments, but we are still at that stage in talking about novels. We have only to take up the literary section of any Sunday paper and count the number of reviews which discuss novels as though they are philosophy, history, sociology, or anything but art, in order to see this.

The confusion in our thinking is helped by the fact that the vast majority of books claiming to be novels—that is, works of art—are not novels in the full literary sense at all. Many are scientific or historical fables; many are rhetoric masquerading as fiction; many are journalism under a thin fictional disguise. The novel has become a type of exposition, a way of putting across facts or exhortations or diagnosis and simply that. Such pseudo novels, if one may use the phrase, have their value. They communicate facts in an interesting way, or persuade people to adopt a point of view which may be valuable, or explain a situation in a helpful manner. They are expository fables. Arthur Koestler's *Thieves in the Night* is an expository fable: it explains a situation, tells how certain people got to be the way they are, and (if one assumes that its facts are correct) throws light on an aspect of contemporary history. Critics rightly criticize it for the degree in which it explains what it sets out to explain and the truth of its picture of contemporary Palestine. Now, expository fables can be told with more or less literary skill. Clarity and cogency of style can add to the effectiveness of expression. Many people write novels to clear their minds, and if in the process they also clear the minds of their readers, it is all to the good. The value of such books lies in the fact that they give useful information or clarify aspects of the contemporary scene. They consist— to use our earlier terminology—of examples, not symbols, and thus are really fables and not novels.[1] They are not even universal fables, but fables illustrating a transient situation. Their meaning will be lost and their value impossible to assess once the situation to which they refer has passed away.

But poetry, in the sense that Aristotle used the word,

---

[1] The previous discussion will perhaps have made clear the difference between a "fable" and a "novel" as those terms are here used. Briefly, it might be said that a fable illustrates concretely what can also be formulated abstractly, while the meaning of a novel cannot be formulated in any other terms. The difference is akin to that between "example" and "symbol."

literature which is the work of the creative imagination, fiction like *Tom Jones, Emma, The Heart of Midlothian, Great Expectations, War and Peace,* to name only a few examples on different scales, does not depend for its appeal or its value on the extent to which it clarifies a contemporary issue: it has those richer and subtler meanings which have been discussed earlier in this chapter. We have become so used to expecting our new novels to be simply expository fables that many of us have stopped looking for a deeper significance even in old novels. So we find Scott and Dickens unreadable since they do not clarify any pressing contemporary problem. In criticizing literature we have forgotten what to look for.

CHAPTER IV

Art and Craft

WHATEVER else can be said about art, it can be safely asserted that it is a form of communication. We may say if we like that every artist is endeavoring to communicate a private vision to his public. The literary artist makes his communication through the medium of words, the painter through color and form, the musician through musical sound, and other artists through other media of communication. Art is the making public (or potentially public) of something that was private. Of course it shares this function with many activities which are not art—with the ordinary use of language in daily life, for example. The uniqueness of art lies in the uniqueness of the kind of thing to be communicated, which in turn requires a uniqueness of expression. Whether the artist begins by being fascinated with his medium or by discovering that he has a set of insights that he can only communicate in an artistic manner, is an academic question. The first poets probably began by simply playing around with the potentialities of speech. The fact remains that a poem or a novel (in the true literary sense of that term) or a painting or a piece of music is the communication of some kind of significance, a significance which cannot be communicated in any other way.

There is no need to be drawn into arguments whether art is essentially communication or self-expression. To express is to make communicable, to put into a public form, and to express oneself simply means to make available to others some private emotion or conception or illumination. Psychologists may of course use the term self-expression in a rather different sense, to indicate the release of something pent up within oneself without regard to the form which that release takes. But it is not art to murder one's wife's lover or to chalk dirty words on walls, though both these activities may be forms of self-expression in this sense. So far as the term can be used of the artist, expression must imply communication, making the internal external, the private public, the personal impersonal; and it can never be merely exclamatory or self-indulgent.

The complexity of the artist's medium will vary. The musician arranges musical sounds in relation to each other in such a way that the pattern of the whole is significant. Significant of what? It is easy but perfectly logical to reply that if that question could be answered, there would be no need for the composer to write his music. He could simply tell us what he meant instead. All we can say is that the significance depends on and is produced by the pattern, the arrangement, the relation of the notes to each other. And it is worth remarking that the medium of the composer is not sound, but musical sound, that is to say, notes as they derive significance from their place in a scale. And we cannot understand the music unless our ear is familiar with the scale. The medium of the painter is in a sense more complex, for he uses not merely color and form, nor even color in its place in a chromatic scale, but color and form in their relation to the colors and forms we find in real life. The pattern of a painting in virtue of which we find it "significant" consists not only of the relation of the parts to the whole but also of what we see on the canvas to what we see in life. This is not to say that painting must be representational, must be a painting *of* something that exists or might exist in the natural world, though of course many paintings do have such a "subject." But it does imply that all painting, from the most directly representational to the purely abstract, depends for its effect not only on the pattern displayed on the canvas but also on the way in which that pattern suggests, comments on, illuminates, or interprets patterns we have experienced or can imagine experiencing in real life. The meaning of the most abstract painting is enriched in some degree by indirect suggestions— sometimes even ironic distortions—of natural objects. The painter may not be aware of any such implications, but the observer will be. The fact that color and form exist in the natural world will always be some kind of enrichment of or comment on painting, whether the painter wants it to be or not. It might almost be said that the more "purely" abstract painting is, the more it becomes an implied criticism of natural form and to that extent will derive some significance from the fact that the world exists as well as the painting.

However that may be, it will be seen that both the musician and the painter create significance by pattern—create it not for themselves but for those others who have learned how to listen to or look at their work. That is to say, they create by communicating, or by making communicable, a pattern, a set of relations, which adds up to a totality of significance. That significance is not expressible in any other way, except indirectly by analogy. Hence the tendency of art criticism to become merely exclamatory or autobiographical. If the exclaimer or autobiographer is sufficiently experienced in and sensitive to the art to which he is reacting, his reaction, though not in itself criticism, will be a valuable indication of quality in the work of art. (The difficulty lies in the adequate interpretation of the phrase "experienced in and sensitive to.")

What, then, of the medium of the writer? It is of course language, and language, unlike musical sound, has a meaning apart from its relation to other parts of a pattern constructed out of the same medium. Pattern to the writer, then, must be something more subtle, in a sense, than it is to the composer (who is concerned only with the relation of the parts to the whole, knowing that the individual notes have no meaning at all in isolation) or to the painter (who, though he may have to consider the relation to the form and color in his work to form and color outside it, is not bothered by having each blob of paint contain a specific meaning in itself). Words have more or less precise meanings, and as a rule the same words used in a unique order by the poet or novelist are constantly being bandied about in different contexts elsewhere. And in each context they will have approximately the same individual meaning. If the artist in words is bound by the pre-existing meaning of those words, how can he hope to achieve anything more than express himself clearly? How can the novelist do anything more significant than the mere journalist could accomplish? Does the difference lie solely in the kind of plot the novelist is able to invent?

The answer to that last question depends to some extent on how we define "plot." If we include in the term the way the action or the situation is handled and presented at every point, we should have to answer the question in the affirmative. But, as we have already seen, this would be to include all the other aspects of effective writing—including "style"—in the term "plot," and such broad definitions are not particularly helpful. Such a definition does, however, suggest the lines on which to approach this whole question of the way the literary artist uses his medium. The good novelist, for example, will use language in such a way that at every point in the narrative the meaning of each unit is sharpened and particularized by its position in the context, by its relation to meanings that precede it and follow it, so that as the story proceeds the narrative line as laid down by the purely semantic meaning of the words becomes, not a single line, but a rich pattern of significance in which the rise and fall of sentences, the length of paragraphs, the verbs and images used in describing an incident all contribute new enrichment to what is being said. The actual intellectual meaning of words thus becomes one element in a complex pattern, for such meaning is continually expanded by overtones and reverberations deriving from the choice and arrangement of words, sentences, paragraphs, chapters; and the plot itself, the relation of the incidents to each other, becomes not a pattern of ideas but a pattern of suggestive words, of a moving picture vitalized at each point by the most effective kind of expression. Words have more than merely intellectual meanings: they have other qualities which, if properly employed, can actually be made to comment on their own meaning as well as on the meaning of other words in the same general context. This is done more intensively and subtly in poetry than in prose, but it is also done in some degree in good prose fiction. To take an example from poetic drama (which combines some of the qualities of prose fiction and lyric poetry): When, in the last act of *Romeo and Juliet*, Romeo is hastening to die by the side of his supposedly dead Juliet, he encounters Paris, the man whom Juliet's parents had provided to marry Juliet. Grown suddenly old in tragic wisdom, Romeo feels this contemporary of his to be of an altogether younger generation, addressing him as "gentle youth" and "boy." Shakespeare does not explicitly indicate Romeo's feeling of age and his attitude to Paris, but the fact that at this point in the play he addresses Paris in those words makes it clear at once, and clear in a way which illuminates suddenly the whole development of Romeo's character and even tells us something more about Paris. Shakespeare is *starting from* the simple intellectual meaning of the words "youth" and "boy," and by their place in the play makes them say very much more than their simple intellectual meaning would indicate. *In literary art, the meaning of words is both more precisely defined and simultaneously greatly enriched by their place in the pattern of the narrative.* In prose, the unit that can be profitably separated in order to have its relation to preceding and following elements in the expression examined is less likely to be the individual word than a larger unit—the phrase, sentence, paragraph. In poetry, where the expression is always more intensive and compact than in prose and enrichment of meaning by position proceeds on a more exacting scale, the critic can, if he wishes, apply the microscope to each individual word and see the new significance it both gives to and receives from its context by the fact of its being just where it is in relation to the others. We are not discussing here grammatical meaning, but comments on that meaning arising from the literary use of language.

Can we say, then, that in a good novel the totality of meaning is enriched by the relation between what the words say considered as scientific discourse and what they are made to say by virtue of the pattern in which they find themselves? Perhaps this is too extreme—or too theoretical? —a statement. We can at least lay it down that literary art, like all art, communicates significance through pattern and that the relation of what the words mean to where they are and where everything else is produces the pattern.

But literature takes for granted our knowledge of life: it is a presentation of an aspect of life which appeals to us because it at once confirms and enlarges our knowledge of it. Is not therefore all this discussion of words and patterns quite beside the point? Is not the significance of a novel, when we really face the truth of the matter, derived entirely from *what* it says, not *how* it says it? Cannot we appreciate the significance of a novel in translation, which would seem to prove this beyond a doubt?

There are several answers to these important objections. In the first place, the translator is translating what the original novelist wrote; he is not freely retelling the story in his own words. Let the reader try the experiment of freely retelling in his own words the story of *The Brothers Karamazov* and see what a ridiculous and incredible tale it becomes. The translator follows the line of the author's imagination at every point, transcribes each image, each analogy, each new turn in the action, and to the extent that he does so without doing violence to the idiom of his own language he reproduces something of the force of the original. Indeed, this brings us back to an earlier point, that style is in a sense an aspect of plot, it is plot in its subtlest aspect, it is the treatment of the action in its most minute parts, and thus a faithful following of the plot at all points cannot but give something even of the style of the original. For we have not been maintaining that in prose the actual sound and rhythm of the individual words make an overwhelming contribution to the meaning of the whole: they do of course make a contribution, and it is not a negligible one, but it is not comparable to the part they play in poetry, where it is very much larger (and for that reason poetry cannot really be translated). In prose the overtones that so enrich the total significance derive largely from the relation of image to meaning (of the concrete picture to the abstract ideas, both often presented by the same words) and from both to the general sweep of the action, and there is nothing here that a skillful translator cannot capture.

There are, of course, different kinds of prose, some more dependent than others on the individual "aura" of words. The novels which translate best are those written in a prose which depends to a minimum degree for its effectiveness on these untranslatable aspects of words. A novelist like Thomas Hardy hews out his flinty sentences with apparent carelessness, and this deliberately cumbersome prose is admirably suited for the large-scale tragedies he gives us. Similarly, the novels of Tolstoy and Dostoyevsky, painted as a rule on a huge epic canvas and dependent on units of expression larger than the individual word, are (it could be maintained) more effectively translated than the works of Flaubert, who suffers in translation more than the reader who knows him only in English might imagine.

As a second answer to the objections raised above, one might simply admit that in translations of novels much more is in fact lost than we often realize. That much of the significance of the original nevertheless as a rule remains is often due to the translator's catching fire by the power of the original and being thus transformed into an artist in his own right. The greater the novel, the more perfect its expression, the more likely a good translator will be to be inspired by it into becoming something of a novelist himself.

Thirdly, we could say that while we must distinguish between a mere fable and a true novel, there is a fable aspect in all good novels—they can, that is, be read by the insensitive not largely as symbolic expression but narrowly as a set of examples. And in fact in many translations of novels, what are symbols in the original become examples in translation. As too many readers have become used to confusing the two, they never notice the difference.

Finally, one might agree with the objector that the significance of a novel is *what* it says, not *how* it says it, but one should add that in a great novel the former includes the latter—that is, the novel says what it says by virtue (and only by virtue) of how it says it. To repeat a point that has been made earlier but which is relevant to the present stage of the discussion, a novel is what it says *and nothing else*. All the combining implications of a well-told story become part of that story, so that it is useless to try to tell anybody who has not read it the "story" of even such a relatively restricted novel as *Pride and Prejudice*.

The novelist is much less likely than the poet to discover his theme simply by contemplating the possibilities of his medium, language. Whereas in poetry it is fairly easy to discover two distinguishable approaches—that of the poet who, like Milton, starts off by having something to say and then brings all the resources of poetic expression to bear on his theme, thereby, of course, re-creating his theme in the process; and that of a poet like Keats, who seems to have started off by being fascinated by what could be done with language poetically employed and to have created his subjects by letting the resources of his medium suggest them to him—in prose fiction it must be very rarely that the subject is created by the medium, as it were. Nevertheless, even in prose fiction it is impossible to separate the "subject" from the way in which it is presented—at least, this is ideally true. It would be true of the "perfect" novel where significance is breathed into the work as it moves by the way in which it moves. It becomes less true as novels become less "aesthetic" and more the simple presentation of a clearly preconceived story in intelligible language. Aesthetic value, so far as that term applies to fiction, can be defined as that unique and expanding meaning generated by the *patterned* use of prose expression, where plot and style flow into one another and determine one another. That combination of recognition and insight, of the "how true" reaction with the "how new," which has already been discussed, is produced only by literature when it is used as an art form and not simply as journalism or as a means of scientific expression.

Pattern by itself does not make literature; it must be the kind of pattern which communicates insight. A mistake made by many contemporary critics, particularly in the discussion of poetry, is to regard subtlety or complexity of arrangement as itself a criterion of literary worth. But pattern in literature is a means to an end, not an end in itself, and the neatest or subtlest arrangement of ideas or images in words is merely a parlor game unless that arrangement is placed at the service of some insight. It is not that the writer has an insight and then develops a pattern which will be adequate to convey it; discussion of which comes first, the writer's sense of significance in what he is handling or his craftsmanship which suggests to him how he can present something significantly, is unreal and in fact meaningless. The point that matters is that what we might call "aesthetic value" in literature does not derive from pattern as such but from the totality of significance to which pattern contributes.

The tendency of modern critics to explain literary value simply in terms of complexity of pattern is understandable as a reaction against the impressionism which long remained —and among popular critics still remains—the dominant critical method. In their revolt against the neoclassic "rules," critics of the last century and even earlier came to judge a work in terms of its effect on themselves and to defend their judgment in autobiographical terms. This tendency, it might be noted, is not a wholly new development created by the "romantic movement"; it has a long and respectable history in literary criticism. But in the last analysis it remains autobiography not criticism, and those modern critics who have repudiated this method in favor of a more objective way of assessing literary worth are certainly right in theory. Their practice, however, is sometimes no more helpful than that of the impressionists. For it must always be remembered that literature exists for the sake of readers, and that its ultimate justification lies in the effect it has on those who are sufficiently experienced in literary appreciation and sufficiently sensitive to that form of art to constitute a proper public. While it is perfectly true that the critic's duty is to discuss "the work in itself as it really is" rather than considerations suggested by the work, the fact remains that the work in itself is of interest and value because it *says* something in a very special way rather than because it *is* something.

Literature is produced by men for men. Its raw material is human experience; its medium is a language identical with or closely related to the language men use in daily intercourse with each other. It depends for its complex of meanings on what men do and feel and are; the illumination it provides is an illumination of experience, of life as lived in our sort of world, not of life lived by angels in Heaven or remote creatures in some distant planet. However superficially removed from our ken King Lear and his environment may be, his story is impressive and moving because it is presented as a symbolic statement (and so an illumination) of what we are made to recognize as fundamentally and essentially an aspect of the human experience we know or know of.

For all our emphasis, therefore, on the part played by pattern in literary art, we must recognize that pattern in itself, however neat or subtle or intelligent, is no necessary criterion of literary value; it helps to create literary value when used in a certain way, and, conversely, when a writer sets out to create an effective work of literary art, he will find that in achieving it he will, consciously or not, have produced a pattern in the process.[1] We have to demonstrate

---

[1] I remember being told as a child that a melody written in "common" or 4/4 time was bound to consist of four bars or multiples of four. Rebelling against this artificial doctrine of rules, I determined to compose myself a melody in 4/4 time without putting it into such a Procrustean bed. But alas, when I counted up the bars of my compositions (I tried several) they always came to eight, or some other multiple of four. Without claiming the slightest value or merit for

more than mere pattern in proving the value of a work of literature, whether it be a novel, a poem, or a play. We must also show what that pattern achieves, show it as a means of obtaining maximum implication out of each unit of expression. Literature, like music and unlike painting and sculpture, is dependent for its effect on the time dimension: a literary work of art expresses its meaning over a period of time, and at each moment—William James's "specious present" where the "already" continuously merges into the "not yet"—retrospect and anticipation combine to set up the required richness of meaning. The pattern in a good novel is in one of its aspects a way of harnessing the time dimension—of making man's enemy into man's servant. What, after all, is "style" except that use of language in terms of which expression in time becomes more adequate and compelling than it could ever be if achieved instantaneously?

In short, pattern must imply more adequate expression, and expression must throw light on some aspect of man's fate. Man's fate is, in fact, directly or indirectly, the sole subject of art. Literature, like all the arts, cannot in the last resort be justified on any but a humanist standard. Literature is worth while because man and his destiny are worth while. This does not of course mean that an artist must have an optimistic view of human nature: some of the world's greatest writers have been pessimists about the nature of

---

my compositions, I might suggest that this experience raised a fundamental point about the nature of art: pattern always exists, but it may exist as a by-product of which the creator is unconscious. I have heard from a distinguished critic a most brilliant analysis of the complex and wonderfully organized plot pattern of *Pride and Prejudice,* which would have astonished Jane Austen.

man. But people do not become pessimistic about things which they feel do not matter, and pessimism is thus one way of indicating concern. What man is capable of—in doing and suffering, of good and evil—is, to the artist, *important*. All great literature breathes a sense of the importance of man's fate, whatever attitude to man the writer may take. Even Swift, tortured by a sense of men's defects into depicting them as disgusting animals or contemptible midgets, is admitting by the very fact that he allows himself to be tortured that what man does and is, is of supreme moment to him.

Those critics, therefore, who, in their zeal for "objectivity," try to nail down some aspect of a work of literature which can be discussed without reference to the relation to life of that work are in danger of missing the one point about literature that really matters. They will, in discussing poetry, develop an ideal of complexity and subtlety of expression which will enable them to discourse brilliantly about John Donne and other poets who, like Donne, deliberately use paradox as an essential part of their technique —and considerably less brilliantly about most other poets. It will *not* enable them to say why we should spend our time reading these complex and paradoxical statements which so excite them. What is the value of complexity and paradox as such? To produce them may be a useful mental exercise, but on what standard can such an exercise be regarded as more than a high-class pastime?

This is not to deny that complexity and paradox play an important part in literature, especially in poetic statement, but the part they play is important only as contributing to the communication of that combined insight and recognition which has already been discussed. If literature is important, if it is worth producing and worth reading and worth training ourselves to read properly, it must be something more than simply a complex kind of expression. Its expression is often (but not always) complex because it has to find a unique way of communicating a unique insight. In that insight lies its ultimate value. In the last analysis, literature is valuable as a kind of knowledge—a unique kind of knowledge about man.

The relation of form to content is one of the oldest of critical problems, but it remains a problem. It is not difficult for the experienced reader to see that the kind of knowledge peculiar to literature becomes communicable only when expression is achieved in a certain way, but while this awareness may suffice for appreciation, it is not enough for the critical demonstration of relative literary worth. The reader knows when he reads that form and content are really one, but the critic finds it necessary to separate them. Critical analysis thus often reveals interesting aspects of the structure of a work without demonstrating that it is therefore good as literature, for structure is a means to an end, or sometimes a by-product of the successful working of the literary imagination: it is not in itself necessarily valuable. A reader sensitive enough to receive the full impact of, say, a good lyric poem could, if he has had any practice at all at that sort of thing, analyze it so as to show its complexity or the paradoxical nature of its expression; and it is even easier to show that a poem which is at once recognized as bad is too obvious or oversimplified in its expression. The extent to which these qualities objectively exist in the poem, and their relation to the experienced reader's reaction to the poem as good or bad, are very different matters. It is not difficult to prove something in the matter of structure and organization if we know in advance what we are going to prove. We find a poem "good" and then proceed to show that it is complex, or we find it "bad" and proceed to show that it is the reverse of complex; but did we find it good in the first place because of its complexity or bad because of its obviousness? This question—relevant both to prose and poetry, but more easily discussed with reference to poetry —is a particularly important one for contemporary criticism. We raise it at this point because it is impossible to raise the general question of the place of structure and pattern in literary expression without recognizing this difficulty. We shall return to it, and examine it more carefully, when we come to discuss the nature of poetry.

What, it might be asked, is the relation of art to mere craftsmanship? Can a man have insight without the skill to express it, or literary skill without any insight for which to make it work? Is it possible to separate art and craft and say that a man may be a good craftsman but no artist?

Clearly, before the artist can proceed to work he must have acquired a certain skill in the handling of his medium. If he is a literary artist, he must know how to handle words— not merely how to express himself clearly and effectively, which is a skill which should be required of every educated person, but also how to bend words to serve richer and subtler purposes. Part of this gift will be innate: there is a kind of creator's sensitivity to language (to be distinguished from the reader's sensitivity) which a man either possesses or does not possess; experience, practice, self-discipline, self-education through trial and error will help him to develop this gift to the point at which he becomes a potential artist. A man becomes a potential artist when he reaches the point where his sense of the potentialities of his medium and his insight into life become fused and each works through the other. At that stage his craftsmanship is not a separable skill which he applies to his work as a painter applies a coat of paint. However much he may revise or correct what he has written, he is concerned with achieving greater objectification for his vision rather than with turning out a more skillfully constructed work. Of course, in practice it turns out that the more adequately he objectifies his vision, the better the job of work he does even from the point of view of simple craftsmanship. The artist must include the craftsman, for unless he is complete master of his craft he cannot see his vision in terms of his medium.

That, at least, would be the ideal situation, where the artist produces a work in which form and content are perfectly merged and the aesthetic value of the finished product is not challenged or confused by rhetorical or scientific purposes. The novel, however, as we have seen, is often an "impure" form; there are often nonaesthetic intentions existing side by side with the aesthetic. The sheer length of many novels makes it impossible or at least difficult for the writer to carry his unified vision in his head all the time. Sometimes the requirements of serial publication play havoc with any such unified vision. While the generalizations made in the previous paragraph are invariably true of the good poet, they are thus not altogether true of the good novelist. Mere craftsmanship is sometimes called in to tide the writer over when his vision temporarily fails. And, separated from its function in the artist's unified conception of the whole, no longer buoyed aloft on the wings of an insight which keeps it from flagging or falling down, craftsmanship sometimes falters and allows the fires of the novel to die down. (The metaphor is mixed deliberately, in an endeavor to make the point by as many analogies as possible.) We find such passages in Dickens and Scott, where they are all the more noticeable in contrast with those other parts of the novel where the fusion between craftsmanship and vision, between form and content, is complete. In some of Scott's later novels, where he is grinding the stuff out in order to earn money, there is a clear gap that shows the light, as it were, between form and content: it is simply craftsmanship put at the service of an independently conceived plot. This is craft and not art, as we can see at once if we put *The Heart of Midlothian* beside *Anne of Geierstein,* or even the first three-quarters of the former novel beside the concluding section.

An artist must be a craftsman, but a craftsman need not be an artist. Many artists operate as craftsmen part of the time and as artists only occasionally. The novelist in particular, because of the length of his work and the length of time necessary to complete it, is liable to descend on occasion to the level of the mere craftsman.

A writer is a craftsman rather than an artist if he first thinks of a subject—whether a plot, an argument, or a description—and then puts it into words clearly and cogently. As we have seen, the artist does not operate in these two separable stages, though sometimes he may seem to. There is, however, another aspect of the relation of art to craft which deserves consideration. Sometimes—though rarely in prose fiction—the mere exercise of a consummate craftsmanship creates, almost in spite of itself, something which might be called art. This can happen in poetry, where the exploitation of the medium for its own sake seems in certain circumstances to result in a true poem. It is not only that the possibilities of the medium suggest and create kinds of insight—though this does happen occasionally in poetry. It is that craftsmanship under certain conditions seems to be able to produce art almost automatically. We can see this most clearly in music, when an exercise written to illustrate, say, the laws of the fugue might result in a perfect work of art. The composer will have to be a musical genius before this will happen, but it does happen: there are occasions when a "study" becomes a "piece." Those of us who have practiced a musical instrument in childhood will remember those occasions when, to our delight, a study emerged as a piece. This suggests that there may exist aesthetic "laws" which, if observed, create significance of their own accord. But this is to become, perhaps, too mystical. It is not everyone in whose hands the miraculous transfiguration takes place. Who knows what subconscious processes go on in the mind of the artist which could explain the apparently automatic functioning of these aesthetic laws? Something like this does, however, happen, particularly in the "nonrepresentational" arts such as music. It happens more rarely in poetry, and whether it can really happen in prose fiction is open to doubt.

CHAPTER V

Literature, History, and Science

THE NOVEL has become so dominant a literary form that anybody who has anything at all to say is tempted to present it as a work of fiction. If we want to criticize the Allied Military Government in Sicily or discuss the problems of contemporary China, we may put our observations into novel form, constructing some characters who do what we want to show A.M.G. officers or Sicilians or Chinese as doing and others who say what we think ought to be said in the circumstances. These novels—or we should rather call them "pseudo novels"—are in part fables, stories illustrating typical actions of the kind the author wishes to draw to our attention as a social critic or a moralist or historian. But they are not wholly fables, for the message is not conveyed simply by the presentation of typical actions which tell their own story but also by making characters in the novel speak directly for the author. The moral of the fable is thus put into the middle of the story. The Second World War produced a spate of such pseudo novels, informing us of all phases of the fighting and praising or criticizing many different aspects of the conduct of the war and the peace.

It would be unjust as well as foolish to attempt to judge these works on the aesthetic standards discussed in the previous two chapters. They are not really works of imaginative literature but disguised history, rhetoric, or autobiography. As such they are useful and valuable to the extent that they are informative or that they lead to good attitudes or actions on the part of readers. It is proper to ask of *A Bell for Adano* whether such things in fact happened in Sicily and to demand that appropriate action be taken if they did. We do not ask such questions or make such demands on reading *Pride and Prejudice* or even *For Whom the Bell Tolls*. Whether *A Bell for Adano* (or, to take another example, already referred to, *Thieves in the Night*) is a good book will depend in some degree on whether the actions described in them are really typical of what did in fact occur. This would not be true, however, of Koestler's *Darkness at Noon*, which is a novel in the true sense. Thus a good novelist can also write a good pseudo novel.

It is odd, when one comes to think of it, that writers should go out of their way to present fact as fiction.[1] One would have thought that they would be more anxious to do the reverse—present fiction as fact. In the early days of the English novel, writers used every possible device to persuade their readers that what they were telling them had actually occurred. Defoe disguised much of his fiction as journalism in his desire to conceal the imaginative nature of his achievement. The very titles of some of his earlier works of fiction suggest the reporter rather than the novelist. In Defoe we clearly see how fiction arose out of journalism and tried to gain acceptance by pretending still to be journalism. This problem of establishing literal veracity remained a very

[1] Particularly odd when, as I am assured by publishers, nonfiction, especially in the field of contemporary history, now sells better than ever before.

real problem to many later eighteenth-century novelists. Samuel Richardson presented his novels in a series of letters supposed to have been written by the characters (but not, of course, seriously claimed as genuine), thus showing how, theoretically at least, he could have come to know the facts he was relating. The discovery of letters remained a popular method of introducing a novel throughout the nineteenth century. It was as though novelists were trying to justify their knowledge of the story they were telling. This pretense, never wholly seriously maintained after Defoe, nevertheless haunted the technique of fiction until the novelist finally asserted his right not only to know everything his characters did and thought but even what went on in their subconscious. The "stream of consciousness" technique is at the opposite extreme from that of Defoe, for here we find the novelist claiming complete omniscience about his characters: he knows even more about them than they could know about themselves. Though this omniscience had long been claimed by dramatists, it was not until the end of the last century that we see it in prose fiction. The "stream of consciousness" technique is the fictional equivalent of the soliloquy in Elizabethan drama, and it emerged three hundred years later.

We now no longer question the right of the author to invent his own characters and actions or his right to claim a greater knowledge of them than any observer could possibly acquire. The situation has so reversed itself since Defoe's day that modern readers actually prefer to have their facts dressed up as fiction. A superficially imposed plot that holds the attention of the "ordinary" reader is often the only device used by the writer of pseudo novels to disguise his truth as falsehood, but it is generally enough. Even that is not always necessary: the mere dressing up of real or typical characters as actors in a novel will often suffice. Readers of fiction have reached the stage where any sequence of events, if they follow each other rapidly enough, is deemed interesting. Action, however monotonous or repetitive, is the great formula (as the radio serials show), and thus in one of its aspects fiction is reverting to the episodic picaresque form which it took in its earliest stages.

It has been said that an age of universal toleration in matters religious and philosophical is only possible when nobody believes anything firmly. It is perhaps true of fiction that it is most generally read and accepted as a legitimate product of man's mind and imagination when nobody holds it to be of any profound value. The fact that the public often prefer their history or biography disguised as fiction does not necessarily mean that fiction as an art form is more highly esteemed today than ever before; it is more logical to assume that they have this preference because history and biography are less valued as history and biography and are regarded merely as quarries from which entertaining stories may be hewn. Far from being suspicious of fiction, as their Puritan ancestors were, today's public prefer that kind of writing to all others—not because they have any clear idea of the nature and value of imaginative literature, but because they have never bothered to think about the matter in that way at all. Fiction, like liquor or tobacco, is a pleasant form of indulgence, and its popularity is due not to its high esteem among the public but to the fact that actually it enjoys no esteem at all. It is liked but not, in the true sense of the word, valued. It might almost be said that novels are popular because hardly anybody takes them seriously.

The battle for art has long been won in theory, but at

considerable cost. Just as we may be tolerant of other creeds because we believe nothing, so we may tolerate art because we value nothing. It is perhaps not accidental that the greatest age of English literature was an age when a large and vocal minority of Puritans objected to stage plays, love poems, and other literary forms to which virtually nobody today would raise an objection. Toleration often conceals indifference or lack of real esteem. It is not good for any aspect of civilization to have no thoughtful enemies, and certainly the universal popularity of fiction is no necessary cause for rejoicing among champions of the arts.

If much of modern fiction consists of what we have called pseudo novels, this does not mean that it is valueless. Many such novels contribute valuable information or interesting ideas. Some of the most thoughtful writing in our time has been presented in this form. The point to be made, however, is that if history or philosophy or social criticism or any other kind of nonaesthetic writing is disguised as fiction it does not thereby necessarily acquire an aesthetic (or purely literary) value and it ought not to be judged as fiction, as imaginative literature. An honest review of a book of this kind might begin with some such sentences as these: "The author of this book has something to tell us about the present state of Germany. He has therefore taken a number of real situations and, under the pretense of writing a novel, has drawn them to our attention and made a number of pertinent comments and observations." The reviewer might then proceed to discuss the book's authenticity as reporting and adequacy as criticism.

It is not, however, always as easy as this. A pseudo novel might "tend toward" true fiction in greater or less degree: certain characters might emerge as more significant than the requirements of the reporting or diagnosis would justify, certain excitements or insights might exceed what is necessary in order to communicate adequately the author's sense of what is noteworthy about the contemporary situation he is describing. The critic would have to discuss and assess these elements, making up his mind whether they really lift the novel into the realm of genuine imaginative literature, and determining the relation between the historical, the rhetorical, and the aesthetic elements in the book. We have conceded, in an earlier chapter, that a novel *may* serve two masters, and that works of Dickens, to take an obvious example, have in fact done so. They are both adequate as novels and, to a contemporary but not to us, illuminating as exposures of specific existing abuses. We have also noticed the difficulties involved in trying to make a novel serve both a minor (strictly contemporary) and a major (universal) function. A critic would in the case of a novel which tried to serve this double function be justified in criticizing it on two standards, though he could not apply them both simultaneously. Most of Steinbeck's novels can in fact be criticized on two standards: Steinbeck is one of the relatively few modern novelists who try to combine contemporary social criticism with the creation of a genuine novel. (There are of course a great many modern novels of social criticism, but most of these are clear cases of what we have called pseudo novels and make no attempt to reach out after some profounder objective.) This kind of combination is quite in the tradition of English fiction, and there is not the least reason to deplore it. But, if we are not to become hopelessly confused in our reading and evaluating, we must have a fairly clear idea of what is really going on.

It is not, of course, necessary to dress history up as fiction in order to make it "literature." It would be useful at this point to inquire into the literary qualities which we do demand of a good history. It is a commonplace of criticism that history can be either a science or an art. That history can be a science, that it can concern itself with the accurate communication of established facts, seems fairly obvious: the discovery and setting down of details of man's past behavior is obviously a scientific activity in the broad sense of that phrase. The interpretation of those facts once they have been discovered and the method of relating them to each other and presenting them in written history raise more difficult questions. We cannot, either by deduction or induction or both, develop laws of history out of the facts we discover about the past in the sense that scientists can frame scientific laws. We may make generalizations about the basic patterns of man's behavior, about historical cause and effect, about the conditions under which civilizations flourish or decay, but these can never be truly scientific (in the sense that the physical sciences are) if only because we cannot experiment with the past in a laboratory, or even observe it: all we can do is ponder over fragmentary records of it. We cannot observe the past in operation, we cannot re-create it at will, and we cannot even be sure that those parts of it of which we have records are in any degree fair samples of the whole. The formulation of historical generalizations is thus largely an act of imagination. We talk about the "historical imagination," and it is a proper phrase, since the historian—to the degree that he is something more than the collector of separate and unrelated facts about the past —must re-create an image of the past imaginatively rather than scientifically. One might call this a philosophical activity, but whatever name we give it the fact remains that the writer of history, as distinct from the mere historical researcher (research is only the first stage for the historian), does not and cannot operate as the writer of scientific discourses does. He has to construct a living picture out of a few dead fragments, and he has to communicate that picture to the public.

The construction of the picture can hardly be called an artistic activity—the historical imagination is not the same as the aesthetic—but its communication will call for some degree at least of the craftsmanship which the artist also needs. The good historian will start with a clear picture in his mind and then proceed to find the words in which to communicate it most effectively. This, as we have seen, is not the way the typical artist works: the artist does not as a rule separate subject and treatment in that cold-blooded way—the two are part of a unified apprehension of the total work which he has in mind from the beginning. Are we to conclude, then, that good historical writing is good craftsmanship, but that it can never be art? An article in a learned review giving the results of some specific piece of historical research might be called science; the second stage, the effective communication of a picture of an age based on previous research by oneself or others, is literary craftsmanship; is there a third stage, at which history can become art?

It might be said that good history tends toward art to the degree that, in communicating the historian's mental picture of an earlier age, language is used in such a way as to expand the events and characters described into something more than merely historical symbols. Without deviating in the least from the facts to which his research or the research of others binds him, the historian, if he is sufficiently gifted, can give to his work a sense of general rather than of local destiny, a sense of the human fate bound up with the fate of the particular age with which he is dealing. Where Gibbon, in *The Decline and Fall of the Roman Empire*, expands the implications of what he says about the later Roman emperors into an ironic comment on the way men use power or on the relationship between individuals and institutions or some other aspect of experience larger than his particular subject matter, he tends to become an artist as well as a historian. If he makes this expansion by explicit generalization, then he is simply acting as a philosopher; but if he allows it to emerge as a result of the way he uses language, then he is acting as a literary artist. Perhaps a historian never operates continuously as an artist, but we find in Herodotus on occasions, in Thucydides and Gibbon fairly frequently, in Michelet and Carlyle very often, passages where a sudden illumination pervades the work and the language seems to be conveying a new insight into man's fate at the same time that it tells its factual story. There can, in fact, be patches of art in history, or shall we say patches that tend toward art. For the large unifying conception that in a work of art pervades the whole and determines at each point the way in which each part is expressed and related to the other parts cannot be assumed to exist in a writer the nature of whose work can only make him an artist in patches. It is in fact theoretically conceivable that a work of history could be throughout a work of art, and perhaps this is true of some of the work of Carlyle, Michelet, Renan and other "romantic" historians. The unifying conception which prompted Thucydides or Gibbon to write was a philosophical rather than an aesthetic one.

All this may sound offensively theoretical, but these distinctions are justified by our experience in reading.

There *is* a difference between good history and good fiction which is quite apart from the fact that fiction is not the report of events which actually occurred. It is a difference in the degree to which the imagination works through language. A writer of fiction could, of course, use historical material in his plot, but if he is primarily a fiction writer his task will be, not to reconstruct the past, but to illuminate the present, and to illuminate the present not by generalized moralizing and the drawing of analogies but by the way in which his material is patterned and presented. The fiction writer who uses historical material imposes a pattern on his material which is not derived from history at all, but from his sense of significance as an artist. If ever those two patterns coincide, then history becomes art.

The reader at this point will probably exclaim that what with pseudo fiction and mere craftsmanship and all the other forms of writing which cannot be classified as art there must be a great deal of writing classified as literature in textbooks which is not really so at all and very little real literary art. But one should recognize that among the many reasons for reading books, the aesthetic one, the communication of that unique combination of recognition and increased insight which has been discussed, is only one among many. It is perhaps the most impressive reason, and a case can be made out for believing that it is the "greatest" books which provide that aesthetic reaction, but it is not in fact a common reason. Most books which are not mere drugs have the value of communicating information. And all information is in some sense valuable. That knowledge as such is good is one of the axioms of civilized man.

Though "mere" craftsmanship does not necessarily imply art, it is not a quality to be despised. The adequate use of language simply as a communicative vehicle has a literary value (in a different sense of the word "literary" than the one intended in the earlier part of this discussion) of its own. To find a writer saying what he has to say in language that fits the thought like a glove is an exhilarating experience, quite apart from any interest we may have in what he is saying. The *value* of this experience is perhaps rather difficult to define. One might say that it is always good for the mind to contemplate the skillful exercise of any craft, particularly one which deals with the translating of ideas into words. The recognition of competence in verbal expression, the sheer pleasure of seeing language handled by someone who is its master and not its slave, is an experience that can be enjoyed only by a reader who has had enough experience in reading and writing to have become sensitive to the medium of language. A sloppy mind cannot appreciate disciplined prose because it has never learned to understand the value of such expression.

This last point might appear obvious, and it might be taken to indicate an unduly patronizing attitude. But it is made in order to stress the close relation between the effective use of language on the level of simple craftsmanship and more general qualities of mind. Good prose and intellectual confusion cannot exist together, as every teacher of composition knows, and a training in verbal expression must begin as a training of the mind. A good composition course is also an elementary course in logic, and it is even more than that, for no adequate study of the relation of words to what they stand for can avoid raising, however obliquely, some of the fundamental questions about man and his nature. Language is a tool developed by man for the communication of what he has to say; to study the tool is to study its uses and to study its uses is to study the user. Thus even this limited aspect of literature can be a humanistic study. This is why the writing of Latin prose was for so long regarded as an essential part of British education. It had a value quite apart from the study of Latin literature: to be forced to contemplate the full meaning of something expressed in your own tongue (whose qualities we too often take for granted) and then illustrate your awareness of that meaning by putting it into another language, a language moreover which has ceased to be a vehicle of daily discourse but remains a rich and vibrant instrument with its potentialities for expression developed by every kind of civilized use in the past—this is more than a linguistic or a rhetorical discipline; it is a training in the mind of man. To translate adequately from one language into another involves recapturing in some degree the thought process of the original writer, and to translate from a living into a dead language (dead only in the sense that it is no longer used in colloquial speech) forces the translator to objectify completely what he has to say, to find language that takes care of all of it, and not to depend on casual contemporary overtones which are liable to arise as much from confused thinking as from a deliberately suggestive use of language.

It is not altogether irrelevant to our main theme to add at this point that the most important part of learning any language is translating into it rather than out of it. In translating out of a foreign language into our own tongue we are apt to proceed by guesswork, to be satisfied with approximations and near misses. Language training as a humanistic study must be accurate or it is nothing. To be able to guess in a very general sense at the meaning of a paragraph is, from the educational point of view, as likely to do harm as to do good, and to assume that it is possible to appreciate the literary quality of a work without paying attention to the precise meaning at any given point is to fall into the philistine error of believing that literary expression is something vague, sloppy, and emotional as contrasted with the clean accuracy of "scientific" discourse. It is, of course, true that the literary artist makes use of aspects of words which appeal to the emotions and that the simpler of these aspects can be recognized by someone who has only a very limited knowledge of the language; but in literary expression there is also a delicacy, a subtlety, an *accuracy* beside which scientific writing appears blunt and smudged.

But it is silly to defend the literary artist by attacking the scientific writer, for they help each other and indeed depend on each other. As the late Professor John Burnet pointed out some thirty years ago, it was the "rediscovery" of classical Latin and Greek in the Renaissance and the feverish linguistic and literary activity that followed which made possible the great scientific discoveries of the sixteenth and seventeenth centuries. These scientific activities could develop only after the Humanists had rediscovered and exercised the classical Latin and Greek tongues which, unlike mediaeval Latin, were languages capable of dealing with scientific thought. This enabled Renaissance scientists to begin where the Greeks left off. (Professor Burnet referred to a translation of Plato's *Meno* and *Phaedo* made in Sicily in the twelfth century which had no influence whatever because it was translated into a Latin jargon incapable of carrying Plato's thought; this throws some interesting light on the relation between literature and science.) The effect on scientists of the exercising of language by men of letters and the effect of scientific discoveries on the literary imagination made the Renaissance what it was—a great scientific and literary age.

The belief that literary and other humanistic studies are somehow inimical to scientific studies is both new and false. It is certainly not borne out by history: the Greeks were if anything more a scientific than an artistic nation and their scientists developed a language that poets could use as much as poets exercised the language for the scientists. In spite of the fact that the way the scientist uses language differs from the way of the artist, science has always proved amenable to literary treatment, has always helped to fire the literary imagination and to develop the insight of the artist, while the artist has often presented tools (not the method of using them but just the tools themselves) to the man of science. The notion that the humanities and the sciences are enemies is a nineteenth-century one; we can make it true by believing it to be true, and by doing so we impoverish both art and science.

To appreciate how art and science can nourish each other is to see how much may be involved in the writing and appreciation of good prose. The literary craftsmanship which is not itself art but is a prerequisite for art affects the very quality of our civilization—the way we think, the kind of expression we give to our thought, the extent to which we recognize confused thought in others. If, therefore, we distinguish between art and craftsmanship and place the former on a higher rung of the ladder, we should not for this reason undervalue craftsmanlike prose. Effective communication of meaning is both a literary and an intellectual virtue, though not necessarily an aesthetic one.

One may therefore read a book simply in order to enjoy the intellectual pleasure of seeing thought clearly and effectively expressed. This pleasure in the *expression* is not the pleasure the scientist experiences when he sees a chemical formula stated in appropriate shorthand; for where mere statements of scientific facts or theories are concerned, the less employment of a communicative skill the better: the ideal "scientific" prose consists of wholly objective symbols with a precise one-for-one correspondence with facts, objects, or relations. The ability to use language (which must be distinguished from the ability to derive intellectual profit from others' use of it) becomes of direct importance to the scientist only when he wishes to *talk about* scientific situations, not to present them. This is not to deny the close relation between literary and scientific activity already insisted on, for talking about scientific situations must precede any scientific discovery and, if the full significance of that discovery is to be developed, it must also follow it. The actual communication of the discovery itself, like the communication of any scientific theory, is often best done algebraically, in symbols. Anything further must be done in language, where the choice of expression becomes important. Thus, though there can be purely scientific communication, there is no such thing as "scientific prose" in any rigid sense. Certain types of communication demand certain types of expression. The less complicated and more wholly objective the matter to be expressed, the simpler and less subtle will the prose be. A description of the flora of Iceland might be written in "scientific prose," in the sense that it might be merely a bald catalogue; it might also be made into something more than that. *The Voyage of the Beagle* is not written in "scientific prose." No adequate account of the significance of atomic fission could be written in a prose which did not demand the highest degree of craftsmanship. Appreciation of the way something is expressed is only possible when the kind of subject to be expressed demands expression through a medium richer and subtler than a formula. When this happens, the *choice* of words and their arrangement become important. As soon as science becomes worth talking about to nonscientists—which is as soon as it becomes concerned not merely with the existence of certain situations but with their significance, and not merely with their application but with their implications—it must seek a medium of expression which requires skill in its proper use.

It is easier to make theoretical distinctions than to recognize them or apply them in practice. One can distinguish mere craftsmanship from art, but in fact there tends to be an element of art in all craftsmanship. Language is a medium more powerful than its users, and to communicate something in language effectively is often to communicate an attitude to the content in the very act of communicating the content. That attitude, conveyed thus obliquely to the reader, may in turn imply a sense of significance, a kind of insight, that cannot be said to be explicit in what is actually expressed. We have here a problem similar to that posed by "functionalism" in architecture or in design generally. There are some critics who would apply the term art to anything which fulfills effectively and without fuss or waste the purpose for which it was designed. This is clearly too inclusive a definition, though it contains a suggestive truth; for the function might be itself a bad or valueless one— slums serve a Malthusian function very effectively, and certain kinds of overdecorated bric-a-brac serve with great success the function of opening the purse strings of certain kinds of idle and moneyed shoppers. Who is to say that these were not the functions intended by their designers? Is the function of a newspaper to attract advertising, to mold public opinion, or to convey information? To accept a purely functional view of art involves deciding between real and apparent functions and probing into problems of intention. Would a nineteenth-century English urban railway station become good architecture if it were discovered that it was *intended* to depress passengers? Would the prose of tabloid newspapers become good literature if it could be proved that its intention was not to convey information but to make a certain kind of appeal to a certain kind of reader? The very posing of such questions indicates that the critic cannot surrender to mere pragmatism.

But there is a significant truth in the functional view. If the function served is either valuable or "neutral"—neither good nor bad in itself—there is likely to arise a certain artistic value in the product which serves it cleanly, economically, effectively; this is as true of drinking cups as of political speeches. This must be because the experience of something which does well what it is appropriate for human beings to do—what is essentially *humanum, ἀνθρώπινον*—is apt to raise all sorts of significant echoes with human implications. *Fata mortalia tangunt,* and to be moved is to see significance— *human* significance—whether it be in the shape of a vessel or the cadence of a sentence. Design brings us from man's behavior to man's fate if in its appropriateness it leads us to contemplate the implications of the actions which the designed object is intended to achieve or assist. To say well something which at a given time it is well to say—it may be only a simple sentence such as "Shut the door" or "The wind is cold tonight"—is to suggest the possibility of a more inclusive meaning than the mere literal expression. And as one definition of literary art might be communication with maximum implication, it might be maintained that all good verbal expression is, potentially or in some degree, art.

One must therefore distinguish between art and craft only to bring the two together again in the end. All analysis is a prelude to the ultimate synthesis, and all theorizing is self-defeating in the sense that its objective is to make itself unnecessary. It is easier to write about the ideal novel than to write it, easier to say what something is "tending toward" than to define exactly what it is. Literary criticism is always exaggerated, always metaphorical, always an oversimplification. At best it is suggestive rather than final. By suggesting what we should look for it may help us to see more clearly, but what we actually observe when we do see more clearly may be something which the critic could not or would not discuss. To say, for example, as we have said in an earlier chapter, that in a good novel style is really an aspect of plot is to state a theoretical truth which, we believe, is certainly helpful to the reader of novels but which the reader may never be able to apply wholly to any given novel. Art is always more complex than any theory about it—more complex and yet more simple, for its meanings are subtle and manifold while its essence is single and even primitive. The critic can do no more than make relevant, but never wholly tenable, generalizations.

CHAPTER VI

Varieties of Literary Value

IT IS, as we have observed, comparatively easy to define the "ideal novel," to describe that cumulative presentation of significance where at each point every unit of expression contributes its quota to the great sum of reverberating meaning. Insofar as we are stressing the organic unity of a work of art we are not making any unique claim for the novel but rather showing how a quality common to all art manifests itself in fiction. If we wish to distinguish between one novel and another, to determine which is the "better," the most effective way is to show the conditions under which fiction becomes art. Narrative must have certain special qualities if it is to come into the larger category of art, and our first concern as critics must therefore be to note those qualities, to show how the realms of narrative and art may intersect, and to throw the spotlight on the intersection. But what about the characteristics of narrative as narrative, those aspects of verbal presentation which are not shared by other media of communication? Are none of these unique qualities of literature valuable?

This question is in a sense unreal, for it is only by exploitation of its unique qualities that any medium can achieve art. Nevertheless, there are certain kinds of expression possible only to certain media, and these, while they may not actually intersect with the realm of art, may yield something of value whose value may not be called "aesthetic" in the sense in which we have been using that term. There is room among the visual arts for mere illustration and decoration, and there is a place in music for program music. An illustration may have independent value as a painting, or it may achieve its full value only in the light of the text it is meant to illustrate. A piece of program music may be appreciated as music independently of the descriptive notes supplied by the composer, or it may require to be taken in conjunction with those notes before it can be heard with full understanding or satisfaction. Every art medium can be used in ways which do not produce art in any complete sense of the word. These ways include more than the mere craftsmanship which we have already discussed. There are many imaginative uses of art media which, through looseness of structure, lack of concentration, progressive shifting of purpose, fluctuations of insight, or simply by deliberate limitation of function, do not achieve that echoing totality of meaning which the reflective reader, listener, or observer comes to consider the characteristic of true art or at least the end toward which artistic expression moves. The great and complete work of art is the exception, particularly in the realm of fiction. But the incomplete work of art is not therefore bad. (One must distinguish between the incomplete work of art and the kind of work which, while it may pretend to be art, is not really art at all.)

If we take up the *Pickwick Papers* and try to discuss it as a novel in the strict sense in which the term has been employed in previous chapters, we shall quickly find ourselves in a state of confusion. For this book is not in fact a novel in that sense at all. It is in essence a collection of short stories, in which the same principal characters keep figuring, where what we have learned about the characters in previous stories gives added point to the adventures in which they are involved. That cumulative significance which emerges in a work of literary art as a result of the way in which it is constructed at each point and the way in which the parts are related to the whole—from the way, in short, in which plot and style merge into each other and become part of one another—is not to be found in the *Pickwick Papers*. Though Dickens does draw on the characterization developed in one incident to enrich the quality of another, this utilization of previous work is not the same thing as the texture of a genuine novel. Our chief pleasure in *Pickwick* is watching how characters run true to form when involved in situations amusingly contrived to provide continuous contrasts between a man's character and his environment. Mr. Pickwick, respectable, stout, benevolent, and naïvely philosophical, is thrown into a succession of situations in each of which his qualities appear incongruous, and it is this incongruity which provides most of the humor. Other characters have their own typical qualities and display them in their relations with each other and with the hero in the situations into which they are precipitated. Such a species of linked short stories depends for its effect on the reader's recognition in each new scene of the increasingly familiar qualities of the characters. Characters are deliberately overdrawn and simplified, and are thrown into as great a variety of incongruous situations as possible. The function of each of the stories that make up the book is to let the characters show their reactions in circumstances where their acting typically will cause the maximum of incongruity or simple fun.

This is not the whole explanation of the appeal of the *Pickwick Papers*. A work constructed as this is can introduce a variety of new attractions in different episodes without having them linked to the main significance of the book as a whole. There can be descriptions of scenes and actions interesting simply for their own sake, accounts of convivial meetings, pictures of old innyards, satires on English institutions, almost anything in fact. Characters may be introduced in one episode without ever reappearing or having any connection with the story, simply in order to be satirized or laughed at or, if they are picturesque, just to be described. Out of this vast collection of anecdotes the reader gets an agreeable sense of life, an impression of human activity divorced from any question of value. Any adequate theory of literature will be bound to take into consideration the kind of satisfaction provided by this kind of writing and to acknowledge its place among the many mansions in the house of literature. (Professor Saintsbury's remark that "in the house of poetry are many mansions" does not fall happily on the ears of a generation of literary critics more puritanical in their tastes than any of their predecessors; but limitation of appreciation is not the same thing as strictness in the application of standards.)

Books such as *Pickwick* must, however, stick to their main general intention if they are not to risk being read for what they are not. Toward the end of *Pickwick,* when Dickens throws that engaging rascal Alfred Jingle into jail and then has the sentimental Pickwick rescue and reform him, a completely new kind of significance is introduced into the book and the spell is broken. An attempt is made to introduce a sense of moral value—and a crude one at that—into a picture of life whose appeal lies in the very fact that it is divorced from all questions of moral value, and the reader is disturbed and annoyed. In the light of this new development all the previous episodes shift a little and become less amusing. If we are to think of *these* aspects of human behavior, the reader might say, then we must reconsider our amusement at Mr. Wardle's elderly sister's unhappy adventure with Mr. Jingle and at the great trial scene of Bardell versus Pickwick; if human failings are to be considered not simply as comic or preposterous but as involving serious moral issues, we had no right to laugh at the Reverend Mr. Stiggins and the lugubrious Job Trotter. Dickens, in fact, as soon as he introduces his prison scenes, rends the fabric of his novel and deprives us of the innocent pleasures which the preceding scenes had afforded us. (He does not, of course, literally so deprive us, because we refuse to take these latter scenes seriously.) He had already almost done this by the introduction of a series of macabre tales at intervals, but these were so overdone that no reader could allow them to cast any real shadow over the story. The scenes in prison, however, and the reformation of Mr. Jingle, we are intended to take seriously, as they concern some of the main characters of the book.

Apart from the anomaly of its concluding scenes, however, the *Pickwick Papers* is an excellent example of a kind of "light" literature which affords pleasure by its humorous and lively pictures of human activity deliberately presented without any cumulative sense of significance emerging from the story. It is picaresque comedy, based on the putting together of caricature and adventure. Its value lies in the kind of pleasure it affords the reader—a pleasure deriving largely from the immense feeling of *gusto* about life which Dickens has packed into the novel: here is man contemplated simply as a lively and fascinating spectacle. We are not concerned with what it all means, but here it is. (In later novels Dickens managed to combine this sense of abundant life with serious social preoccupations: it might be said that the scenes in the debtors' prison achieve this combination at the end of *Pickwick,* but, as we have pointed out, what we have here is a juxtaposition, not a combination.) It is at the other extreme from the novels of George Eliot or Dostoyevsky, in which the novelist's concern is with the *significance* of it all. Unfortunately, this kind of picaresque comedy, though it has a long history in English literature, is not a common form today: some types of detective story come fairly close to it without, however, communicating anything like the sense of life in action which we get from Dickens.

One must distinguish this kind of picaresque comedy from "true" comedy, and the distinction can be readily seen when we put Jane Austen's *Pride and Prejudice* beside the *Pickwick Papers.* The former is a genuine novel, in which at each point expression and construction enrich the cumulative significance of the whole. It is comedy in the sense that it approaches the question of the relation between the sexes from the point of view of a worried mother trying to marry off her daughters. This is a comic approach, but the subject continues to gather new and richer meanings at every turn. Comedy brushes the sleeve of tragedy and half turns for a moment to watch it recede. Nothing could be more comic than the portrait of Mr. Collins, but in the possibility of his marriage to Elizabeth and in his eventual marriage to Charlotte Lucas a host of sad and serious implications are set going beneath the surface of the novel. Indeed, it is hardly too much to say that the whole problem of women's helplessness in a society devised by men is obliquely raised, or at least that this note is sounded, faintly but disturbingly, beneath the gay orchestration of the plot. We find this even if we confine our attention to Mr. and Mrs. Bennet, whose relations seem on first sight to be merely amusing. Mrs. Bennet had captured her man early, and assured herself of a proper context for her gentility. (She is not, it is true, as genteel as she might be—but that only means that she has a tendency to tell the truth about the economic objectives pursued by members of her class.) She had successfully fooled Mr. Bennet when she was young enough for her beauty to outweigh her silliness, and Mr. Bennet spent the rest of his life regretting it. It had clearly been no genuine love match, but a match between cool self-interest and male susceptibility. And silly though she is, Mrs. Bennet is realistic enough to know that by hook or by crook her daughters must be properly married off before their looks begin to fade. A genteel upbringing is the worst possible equipment for life unless you secure a wealthy husband. How much more necessary is marriage to the Bennet girls than to their servants! The pathetic Miss Bates of *Emma* remains an awful warning.

Yet the atmosphere of Jane Austen's novels does remain that of comedy. There is almost what might be called a ballet movement in many of them—or perhaps something between a ballet and a Mozart opera. The characters circle round each other with appropriate speeches and gestures, and occasionally a grotesque like Mr. Collins joins the dance as a symbol of one kind of fate that threatens the dancers. Jane Austen's world is a woman's world, and in it the male characters are simply symbols of the different fates in store for women.

It is a stately dance on the lawn—but all around there are the dark trees, the shadows. And if you do not dance well, if you have not been able, by the end of the day, to secure a permanent partner with whom to walk off the lawn, you are left, when the sun sets, alone amid the shadows. We are never allowed to forget that possibility, never allowed to forget what a serious business this dancing is. One false step can be fatal. One must keep one's equilibrium on a razor's edge, with the fate of Charlotte Lucas and Miss Bates (to say nothing of that which overtook Lydia Bennet) waiting on the other side.

All good comedy is potential tragedy and, if we follow up all the clues, it is to tragedy that we shall come. And this is not any indictment of the comedy in the sense that prison scenes in *Pickwick* give rise to criticism of Dickens: the tragedy that lies far beneath Jane Austen's novels is part of those infinite reverberations which every good literary work sets up. What happens to *The Merchant of Venice* if we pursue Shylock to the bitter end or even contemplate the future of Bassanio and Portia? What will happen to Ferdinand and Miranda when they leave the enchanted island and go back to a corrupt world? The author of a comedy does not allow these overtones to come out in the open, as it were: in comedy, as opposed to tragedy where the meanings are encouraged to echo away into infinity, there is a "baffle" set up to absorb some of the overtones— but they are not completely absorbed, and the reader cannot escape them entirely.

The *Pickwick Papers,* then, is not comedy in the full

literary sense: its value derives from the *complete* blocking of reverberations, so that we get a sense of life without a sense of its significance. If we ask ourselves how Dickens manages to achieve this effect of life, we shall find that this depends partly on his narrative style—which manages to convey continuously the impression of a good-humored observer—and partly on his choice of incidents. The literary skill here consists in the author's ability to present vivid images, his lively and energetic language, his ear for effective dialogue, all put at the service of a rich inventive power. If the result is not the highest form of art, it is at least a very respectable achievement, and one capable of being enjoyed in a greater variety of moods than those in which we welcome the greatest masterpieces of the world.

If in the *Pickwick Papers* we have an example of a novel in which the unity imposed by the plot (such as it is) is no real unity and the separate incidents fall apart into a number of short stories illustrating the increasingly familiar psychology of the actors, we have in James Joyce's *Dubliners* the opposite situation—a collection ostensibly of short stories which in fact combine to form a highly complex yet unified work. The separate stories can be read and appreciated individually, yet their full significance emerges only when each is considered in the light of all, and the picture of Dublin that is cumulatively built up is allowed to form itself. Joyce planned and arranged these stories with great care—no other novelist in English was so concerned with the design of his completed works and the relation of the parts to the whole in each—and *Dubliners* is most adequately read as a presentation of the essence of Dublin life presented discursively through the arrangement in a particular order of a series of symbolic incidents and situations.

The works of Jane Austen and James Joyce (to take as widely differing examples as possible) thus illustrate a fully artistic or aesthetic use of narrative, while a novel such as the *Pickwick Papers* only partly does so. There are many other valuable kinds of narrative which do not employ the medium in a "fully aesthetic" way. It is even open to question whether the greatest works of fiction must always be those in which the vision is single and unified and the parts related to each other with complete inevitability. Ideally, the greatest works are also the most perfect—not because perfection of form is a separate quality from "greatness" in any other adequate sense, but because the kind of insight which art communicates is bound up with that fine organization of the total communication which we recognize perhaps most immediately in a lyric poem. But the task of a novelist is in a sense harder than that of the lyric poet, and in a sense easier. It is harder because he has to draw together into a unity so many more elements, because he must work more discursively and less intensely, because he has the problem of holding his imaginative conception in his mind for a longer time; it is easier because the nature of the form he has chosen allows him to spread himself more, to cast his net wider, to indicate relations explicitly rather than fuse them more or less instantaneously. A novel works on the reader over a considerable period of time, and its pattern can therefore be broad and the units of effective communication relatively coarse (the whole paragraph, perhaps, rather than the individual image). A novelist intent on presenting a rich and significant illumination of experience, eager to reach out to all the implications underlying the particular area of human fate which is his ostensible subject, will welcome the opportunity given to him by the more discursive nature of the form he is using to add to his meaning, to push the limiting frontiers of expression ever further and further back, by occasionally putting in a scene viewed from a different perspective or by reinforcing vision with fable, a more general symbolism with a more specific and *vice versa*. Dostoyevsky works this way in *The Brothers Karamazov,* and most of the great English novelists have availed themselves in some degree or other of this liberty to go a little outside the immediate structure of their work in order to compensate for the fact that a novel reader cannot hold everything in his head at once and needs to be prompted by some such device to put the parts together in the proper way. Thus, while formal perfection is the aim of all art (as a means, not as an end in itself) there are kinds of art in which formal perfection in itself tends to be stultifying, because the form is of a kind in which the perfect structure can never be seen all at once and some compensating devices must therefore be introduced. We have only to put *The Heart of Midlothian* beside *Emma,* or one of the great novels of Tolstoy or Dostoyevsky beside *Madame Bovary,* to see that the more ambitious novelist tends to be less scrupulous formally. (Of course in a sense Flaubert is "more ambitious" than Scott or Tolstoy, but not in the sense that he wants to communicate more comprehensively a significant set of truths about man.) Perhaps it might be said that the greatest novelists of all are those who are so obsessed and fascinated by the aspect of life with which they are dealing that they will sometimes go outside the form of their work to make sure the reader feels the full impact of everything the author wishes to say. Shall we say that the great novelist takes human frailty into account more than the great lyric poet?

A writer may fail to be a perfect artist through excess of greatness, as it were; but it should be remembered, too, that a limited genius may produce work which might fall anywhere in the scale between mere craftsmanship and significant art. He may write books whose value lies *merely* in liveliness, or oddity, or irony, or character portrayal, or suspense, or humor of one kind or another, or any one of innumerable qualities, and our literature would be poorer without them. The scale is a large one, and value of one kind or another can lie anywhere within its range. All we ask is that a book does not pretend to be what it is not. If we cast our minds over English literature and think of the rogue literature of the Elizabethans, the seventeenth-century character writers, the de Coverley papers, *Rasselas,* the "gothic" novel, the novels of Thomas Love Peacock, *Alice in Wonderland, Erewhon*—to go no further and to confine ourselves to prose narrative—we can see all kinds of literary works, none full-blown novels in the complete aesthetic sense, but each having a very real value, each falling somewhere in the scale between mere craftsmanship and great fiction.

One could single out any number of these intermediate literary types—the character sketch, the ironic fable, the moral tale, or other varieties—but one perhaps worth pausing at briefly is the fantasy, that not very common but most interesting kind of writing in which the author tries to break down the reader's normal expectations about how events follow one another, perhaps in order to make him reconsider his expectations more carefully, perhaps in sheer disgust at the way things are arranged in this world, perhaps out of pure playfulness. This breaking down of the reader's expectations often produces a kind of moral refreshment: the reader finds himself in a world where normal responsibilities do not exist, and as a result he may be able to discover new angles of approach to things. Fantasy may be written with the deliberate intention of suggesting a moral order or a kind of significance in life wholly different from anything generally accepted or imagined; it might be said that insofar as Blake wrote fantasy that was its purpose. It may be an implicit—perhaps even an unconscious—criticism of the way the world works with us: *Alice in Wonderland* continues to delight us (whatever added insight into its origins we may derive from Freud) because it is in a sense a continuous criticism of experience as we know it and of the laws of thought as we accept them. It is worth noting that fantasy appears either when community of belief is so generally established that fantasy will immediately be recognized for what it is and never confused with reality, or, conversely, in a transition period when community of belief has been shattered and the writer turns to fantasy because of the difficulty of deciding what is real and what is fantastic. The latter type of fantasy—some of Franz Kafka's writings could be so described—is rarer and more difficult to produce than the former. It results not so much from a deliberate design to be unreal as from a refusal to decide what is real and what is not, and different readers may see different degrees of reality in it. It represents a relief from deciding what is reality, as distinct from the former kind of fantasy which is simply a relief from reality.

All arts have their by-products which can be played with.

Literature as pure play is particularly common in the English language. In verse we have forms like the limerick and the "clerihew" or the kind of forms employed by Ogden Nash—forms which take for granted the existence of a body of serious literature and operate with deliberate lack of seriousness against that background. Such literary activity is a form of parody, and parody can only be appreciated by those familiar with what is being parodied.

Every art is capable of laughing at itself, and the laughter, as well as being pleasant for its own sake, often has the merit of pointing out the narrow line that divides the sublime from the ridiculous. The nonsense verses of Edward Lear represent a genial mockery of serious literature, and as we read we laugh at ourselves for our interest in "great books." To be forced momentarily into the role of the philistine is healthy for any serious reader. We must mock at our own serious preoccupations sometimes in order to preserve our sanity. There is in English a peculiar tradition of self-mockery which is most enjoyed by those who appreciate literature most profoundly.

The varieties of these intermediate forms of literature are innumerable. Some of them—satire, for example, which itself has numerous branches—represent such important phases of literary activity that it is impossible to treat them with any adequacy in a brief general chapter such as this. Satire can range all the way from rhetorical abuse to the subtlest indication of disparity between the real and the ideal, and, if what we have called the "symbolization" is adequate, it can reach out beyond its immediate objective to stand as a permanent illumination of types of human weakness or folly. Between the craftsmanlike insult (such as Dr. Johnson's famous letter to Lord Chesterfield) and the profounder kinds of satire (from Norman Douglas' *South Wind* to Swift's *Gulliver's Travels*) lies a richly variegated field.

Each age tends to develop its favorite minor form of literature. The detective story—a highly conventionalized form in which death is a *datum* without significance in itself and where the main interest lies in the adroit successive exhaustion of possibilities until the point is reached where the most improbable becomes the only possible—has been popular for some time, and has developed many interesting subspecies. The detective story presents a framework into which almost any depth of literary expression can be fitted, but of course a detective story which has a literary value greater than that provided by suspense, excitement, and the intellectual pleasure of following the solution of a complicated puzzle must be something more besides. In one of its aspects, the *Oedipus Rex* of Sophocles is a detective story—and one to put most modern practitioners to shame for sheer unexpectedness of the solution, for the detective finally proves himself to have been the murderer—and *Hamlet,* at least until the end of the play-within-a-play, could also be so described. But though tragedy can base itself on a detective story framework, the pure detective story is never tragic: the murdered person must be someone with whom the reader has little concern, and the final fate of the murderer must leave the reader untouched. Nevertheless, a well-constructed detective story can be as neat an exercise in a purely formalized kind of writing as an Elizabethan sonnet; and, like the Elizabethan sonnet, it need be nothing more, though it may be a great deal more.

Another minor kind of fiction which is always popular is the simple adventure story, a type of writing which, while demanding some of the skills of the genuine novelist, need not achieve that richer symbolization which accounts for the appeal of imaginative literature in its highest form. In the adventure story, the reader is invited to identify himself with a hero and follow him through a succession of exciting dangers to ultimate security. The nature of the adventures described constitutes the real appeal of such a story, and style is important only to the extent that it presents the adventures clearly and vividly. There is a "subject" communicated through suitable language, and we can separate the content from the craftsmanship. We can even put the content into another medium and it will lose little of its effect. (The narrative of *The Thirty Nine Steps* told in other words than Buchan's, or put on the screen as Hitchcock put it, has almost the same appeal as the original story.) As with the detective story, the adventure story is not necessarily a good novel in the full aesthetic sense, but many a novel which is good in that sense is also a good adventure story. There are even adventure stories which set out to be simply good "escapist" tales but are raised to something more by a fusion of style and plot; *Treasure Island,* as we have noted, is among this group.

One might continue indefinitely listing what could be called minor or intermediate types of literature, varieties of writing which display skill or virtuosity in some form or other but which do not attain to the status of literary works of art in the sense we have defined earlier. There is every reason why such varieties of writing should be produced and enjoyed. In the realm of art the minor is not the enemy of the major nor is the good the enemy of the great. Pretentiousness rather than lack of scope is the enemy of great art: we have nothing to fear and a great deal to gain from a deft minor poet like Matthew Prior, but a great deal to fear from such productions as Blackmore's *Prince Arthur* or Wilkie's *Epigoniad*. Wherever language is used with skill and integrity, some kind of value, some legitimate pleasure (and surely all pleasure that is not harmful is valuable) results. It is both proper and necessary for the literary critic to construct a scale of values with reference to which it can be seen that *Hamlet* is a greater play than *The Importance of Being Earnest* and *Tom Jones* a greater novel than *The Innocents Abroad*. But what is good of its kind remains good of its kind, not an inferior version of a better kind. One must therefore distinguish sharply between what is inferior literature in the sense that it occupies a lower rung in the ladder of literary "kinds," and what is inferior because it does not achieve successfully what it sets out to achieve. This is a commonplace of literary criticism, and is expressed as well as anywhere in Pope's *Essay on Criticism:* "In every work regard the writer's end." But it is the commonplaces of criticism which tend to be forgotten or at least disregarded in practice, and it is worth emphasizing once again the difference between good minor works and bad works before proceeding to discuss certain common kinds of badness in literature, and especially in fiction.

II

As we have noted, the commonest kind of fiction today is the journalistic or historical record cast into the superficial form of the novel. Such works, of course, have a part to play in our culture, often a useful and sometimes an important one. Though the kind of imagination and literary skill which has gone to make them is very different from that which produced *Le Rouge et le noir* or *To the Light-house,* these works are not necessarily unimaginative or unskillful. We can, however, say of most of such works that they are presented to the world in a form which is not really justified by their nature. If people prefer to read history when it is presented as though it were fiction, if they will only read an interpretation of Chinese society or Russian ideology when it is superficially connected with the relations of a pair of lovers, there is no reason why we should not allow them to have this sugar-coating to the historical or philosophical pill. We are back with the critics of the Renaissance, back to Sir Philip Sidney's view that the function of literature is to "teach delightfully" and that literary devices are lures to entice pleasure-loving readers to some serious thinking. But the devices in such works are not "literary" in more than a very superficial sense. They are superimposed on the real historical or sociological or philosophical work and play no organic part in its presentation. They bear the same relation to the real meaning and significance of the book that the sugar-coating on a cough drop bears to its effectiveness.

The first duty of the critic of fiction, therefore, is to decide whether the work under consideration belongs essentially or only superficially to that category of literary art which we call prose fiction. When he has done this he will be able to see clearly just what he is assessing, and be able to pass a value judgment with some realization of the kind of values with which he is dealing.

Though it is probably true that the great bulk of "serious" fiction now produced consists of psuedo novels rather than genuine works of literary art, we cannot ignore the large numbers of novels which are written purely for entertainment and which claim to be genuine works of imaginative literature. When these are bad—and far too many of them are—we cannot substitute another standard on which they turn out to be good after all. The faults are real faults, and the critic should be able to detect and classify them.

The commonest of these faults is the construction of a novel out of stereotyped patterns. Though it may be true that there is only a limited number of situations on which the novelist can draw in building up his plot, the novelist must make a situation wholly his own by the manner in which he apprehends it and in which he gives it compelling life through his own imagination. If fiction develops significance through style and structure, then that style and that structure must be uniquely conceived in terms of the novelist's own vision, of his own sense of significance in the situations he presents. One cannot borrow other people's insights in writing fiction. Yet that is precisely what so many of our popular novelists try to do. It is not a question of borrowing mere plots, but of borrowing ways of handling plot, methods of presenting situations, even down to the smallest stylistic devices. Nothing illustrates more clearly the point made earlier about the relation of style to structure than the degree to which the stereotyping of the handling of situations leads inevitably to the stereotyping of style. And a stereotyped novel is a dead novel, an inert and valueless account of events which did not in fact occur. It is a commonplace that a writer of imaginative literature must have originality, but it is the *kind* of originality that matters. The originality we demand of the genuine novelist is something much more important than mere originality of plot—it need not, in fact, include originality of plot. Before a novelist can make his insight communicate itself cumulatively through the way in which the story is told—through style *and* structure, which, as we have seen, flow into one another—he must himself see every part of his material in its relation to his own vision, must see strictly why *this* word, *this* paragraph, *this* incident, *this* character must be precisely as it is. His methods may or may not be traditional: the important point is that he should adopt them out of a sense of compulsion and necessity. A second-hand insight is a contradiction in terms, and by the same token second-hand methods of expression are equally out of the question. The cliché in literature is not confined to words and phrases: it is an all-pervasive vice, resulting from an attempt to profit directly by other people's insights. And the most disturbing part of it all is that publishers and, to an even greater degree, magazine editors actually encourage this kind of dead writing by demanding certain stock situations and stock methods of handling them on the part of fiction writers.

The problem of the cliché is perhaps better studied in poetry than in prose, for in poetry it jumps more immediately to the eye. Although a discussion of poetry is reserved for the chapter that follows, it might be useful at this point to raise a question which, illustrating the nature of the cliché in poetry, at the same time throws some general light on the whole problem of stereotyping in literature.

It is said that a student at an American university once sent to a well-known New York publisher some half-dozen sonnets of Shakespeare with a note saying that these were the student's original poems and he would like to have the publisher's opinion with a view to having a book of his poems published. Would the publisher tell him what he thought of these samples? The publisher, not recognizing the sonnets as Shakespeare's but seeing at once that they were written in an Elizabethan style, replied that the poems were weakly imitative and showed no original talent. He advised the student to give up the idea of being a poet. Was the publisher justified?

In a sense, of course, the publisher was quite right. These were not poems that a modern poet, giving expression to his own sensibility in his own terms, would be likely to write. The inference was that he had imitated older poetry and had no original talent of his own. But does this mean that Shakespeare's sonnets are good only if we keep in mind that they were written in the sixteenth century, and if we imagined them written today we must consider them bad? Must we know when a poem was written before we can judge it? To make such a claim would, of course, be to abandon all real standards. But what is the alternative?

We can clarify this problem by noting that if a contemporary writer used images, metaphors, phrases, or any other piece of poetic apparatus precisely as they were used by an Elizabethan poet they could not be likely to have arisen directly from his own personal struggle to fit his language to his vision and to communicate the latter through the former, and would therefore lie in the poem as inorganic phrases not really *growing* in their context. The fact that they did not so stick out in the sonnets which the student sent to the publisher would mean one of two things—either that they were genuine Elizabethan poems, or that here was a curious freak character whose sensibility actually operated in Elizabethan terms. Whichever of these two explanations the publisher accepted, he would have had to admit the merit of the poems. But in order to see that the Elizabethan devices were organic to the poem he would have to read it with great care and sensitivity, he would have to have acquired, through much experience in reading poetry, through the training in reading which comes only through such experience, an awareness of genuineness and falsity in poetry, an ability to distinguish the organic from the inorganic image. If he read the poems hastily, noticing only that they were full of what appeared to be Elizabethan echoes, he would have been justified in dismissing them as merely imitative. If he read them with care and with the concentration that the reading of poetry demands and still came to that conclusion, then he was not a good reader of poetry—which is to say that he was a bad critic and his judgment was wrong. Ideally, he should have been able to see that they were written either by a true Elizabethan poet or by someone who genuinely felt and thought, in relation to language, in the way the Elizabethans felt.

The problem is, of course, rarely as subtle as that. Most bad poetry owes its badness to its following of stereotyped ways of feeling and of expression, which can be easily recognized. A modern poet who compares his sweetheart to a rose is probably not making the comparison out of any passionate awareness of his own, out of any personal reaching out for an image adequate to express his insight, but that does not mean that the spontaneity and lyrical quality of Burns's poem beginning "My love is like a red, red rose" have now disappeared. The relation of the image to its context should tell whether it is genuine or artificial.

All this applies equally to fiction, but there the units are often less clear-cut than the individual image and to some people not so easily recognizable. It all comes down to the question of *individuality of apprehension* of one's subject with respect to the medium one employs in expressing it. Even this way of putting it is misleading, because, as every experienced reader knows, in the last analysis there is no such distinction between form and content, between what is expressed and how it is expressed, in a work of art. It is often necessary, in discussing literature, to make distinctions in order later to make one's point clearer by denying them.

A less common, though by no means rare, kind of fault in fiction is simply lack of truth—not lack of literal truth, for of course the fiction writer is concerned with the Aristotelian "probable" rather than with the possible or actual, but contradictions within the plot as imagined and presented. (It is even possible for the style to contradict the plot by trying to impose, through the method of expression, a greater meaning on the situation than the situation, as conceived by the writer, can really bear.) A novel like James Barrie's *Little Minister* contradicts itself in this way: as many critics have seen, it is a tragedy that becomes a comedy because the author lies. "*The Little Minister* ought to have ended badly," wrote Robert Louis Stevenson to Barrie in 1892; "we all know it did; and we are infinitely grateful to you for the grace and good feeling with which you lied about it." Stevenson's gratitude was probably assumed out of friendship for Barrie; he saw the main point about the book quite clearly. There are many ways of lying in fiction, and these lies of the imagination are much more serious than the literal lies told by bad journalists or inaccurate historians.

A very common fault in contemporary fiction is that it provides recognition without insight. Good journalism, as we have seen, provides recognition without insight, but when fiction gives us this it is difficult to see what value it has. To describe the adventures of an imaginary family as though they were simply the family next door, without any interpretation through style, is a somewhat pointless activity, and one surprisingly common on the American radio. This is to be distinguished from the meticulous realistic detail of an early novelist like Defoe, who builds up detail in order to convince, not simply in order to arouse fellow feeling. We admire the sheer craftsmanship with which he communicates a sense of authenticity and Defoe is at his best—and he moves from mere craftsmanship into art—where his careful realistic touches are applied—as they are in *Robinson Crusoe*—in a remote and unfamiliar situation. Out of the juxtaposition of the familiar and the unfamiliar emerges a whole view of life. Interest in the routine daily life of a family identical with one's own is not a literary interest: it results from the desire to be reassured that one's neighbors are the same as oneself.

Mere sensationalism must be added to our list of fairly common faults in fiction. To present a situation merely because it is horrid or outrageous is not in itself a literary activity. The horrid and the outrageous have their place in literature; they are possible components of both tragedy and comedy; but merely to shock or excite is not a function of literature. The commonest type of sensationalism in modern fiction is sex sensationalism, of which "spicy stories" are the most typical form; but this type takes many more pretentious though no more valuable shapes in full-length novels.

One of the most commonly recognized faults in fiction is sentimentality, and this is a kind of falseness so that it is really a subcategory of the fault already discussed. Barrie's *The Little Minister,* which we took as an example of falseness, is also a classic example of sentimentalism. There are, however, many kinds of sentimentalism. One kind can be defined as the development of an action, in accordance with an unconvincing and evasive view of what life ought to be, to a point inconsistent with the nature of the action previously presented. Another kind is the use of an emotion, wholly disproportionate to the events which aroused it, in order to solve problems soluble in no other terms. A writer might, for example, bring together a number of undesirable characters and put them into relations with each other which demand a tragic or perhaps only a sordid outcome, and then empty a bath of love over them, as it were, in which all difficulties are apparently (but not really) dissolved. This is a favorite device of Saroyan in his more recent work, and Steinbeck has shown an unhappy fondness for similar methods in his later books. Sentimentality of this kind, though it is seen most clearly in the organization of the plot, inevitably leaves its mark on the style too.

A term commonly used by conservative critics is "decadence." Has it any real meaning when applied to fiction? This is partly a question of terminology: decadence generally resolves itself into a combination of other faults. Sentimentality, for example, is a kind of decadence, and so is sensationalism. The combination of the two is what is generally meant by the term. It would not, perhaps, be unfair to call Steinbeck's *Wayward Bus* (his least effective novel) decadent, for it combines sentimentality with what appears to be a perverse sensationalism which the reader finds it very difficult to take seriously. It is arguable whether a novelist's picture of life can be itself "corrupting." The presentation of vice in a purely sensational way perhaps deserves that title. Some critics attacked Edmund Wilson's

Memoirs of Hecate County as decadent and corrupting. It certainly is not the latter, as it makes vice anything but attractive. It is, however, a picture of unimportant aberrations which are given neither interest nor significance (but only a sort of clinical clarity) through style, and so perhaps belongs to the category of adequate minor writing rather than of genuine literary art.

There are certain kinds of pretentiousness often found in novels that can be grouped together as representing a single kind of fault. It is quite common to find a novelist trying to pretend that he has written a real novel when in fact he has not, using ponderous devices disproportionate to the effect aimed at or achieved, or trying to add significance through excited comment rather than through the way in which the material is presented and organized. Critics are sometimes impressed by this at first reading, but as the book takes shape in their minds afterwards they see their error. The commonest type of pretentiousness is simply disproportion between style and plot: instead of both being degrees of the same thing the former is used to bolster the latter, and the results are generally disastrous.

There are many worthy novels, solidly built but dead, which seem to have avoided all these faults yet which stubbornly refuse to come alive. It is sometimes difficult to see what has happened here, and in fact this phenomenon may have many different causes. It is most likely, however, to have been caused by an initial failure of that creative imagination which alone can give what Henry James called the sense of *felt life* to a work. Novels, if they are good novels, are never merely literary exercises: they are all, in the last analysis, expressions of the author's excitement about life, about experience. The literary imagination is bound up with that excitement and cannot exist without it. That combination of recognition and insight, which we have claimed as the unique effect of imaginative literature, comes with liveliness and a sense of life. It is not enough for the artist to combine a skill in his medium with a wish to interpret experience—he must first be fascinated by experience, and his interpretation must communicate that fascination.

CHAPTER VII

The Nature of Poetry

POETRY is today much less read than prose fiction, and those who do read it generally have a clearer idea of why they do so than those who read novels. For the ordinary reader, poetry is simply the rhymed and metrical expression of agreeable commonplaces. We have only to turn to the poet's corner of the small-town newspaper to appreciate this. The sentiment expressed must be optimistic and "elevating," the form must be simple, the metre must be regular, and there must be a simple rhyme scheme. This is not necessarily a preposterous view of the nature and function of poetry: it is a simplification (and perhaps a vulgarization) of an attitude which goes very far back in the history of criticism and which has found distinguished exponents. It is, however, an unsatisfactory view in the light not so much of the history of criticism as of poetic practice. It has often been said that we are living in an age of disintegrating public belief, and there are, of course, many disadvantages attendant on that state; but such a period at least forces the thoughtful reader of literature to distinguish between expressions of belief and expressions of attitude— forces him, in fact, to read poetry as poetry and not as philosophy or ethical teaching. We read Donne's *Divine*

Sonnets without accepting Donne's theology: we must ask ourselves therefore why we do read them. A skeptical age is a good period in which to pause and reflect on the nature and value of all imaginative literature, and especially of poetry, which, because of its obvious difference in form from other kinds of serious writing, is too often taken to have a uniform kind of content or at least a uniform purpose.

Our generation has produced many readers who appreciate Donne and Hopkins without agreeing with either, and who have as a result been led to develop a view of poetry (and sometimes a way of writing poetry) at the furthest remove from the Horatian ideal of delightful teaching. Nevertheless, these remain a small minority of the reading population, and the gap between "serious" or "high-brow" readers of poetry and the ordinary "book lover" is much wider than that between readers of different kinds of fiction. This may be because disintegration of public belief, however widespread its effects and however frequently deplored, does not actually affect the views of more than a small minority: most people perpetuate, however dimly, traditional attitudes and look to poetry to confirm them. (It may be noted that in the popular mind the didactic function of literature has never been abandoned for poetry to the extent that it has for prose fiction and other literary forms.) It is the self-consciously advanced minority who have in our time developed further than at any other period in the history of literature the view that poetic statement differs in the way it uses language and the kind of truth it seeks to express from every other kind of verbal expression. That view has been applied not only to contemporary poetry but to the whole *corpus* of poetry in Western literature, and it is perhaps the most characteristic (if not the most significant) contribution so far made by the twentieth century to literary criticism.

Whether one agrees with all the implications of the characteristic modern view or not, one cannot help being influenced by it, nor can one discuss the nature of poetry without taking it into account. We shall endeavor toward the end of this chapter to assess some aspects of modern poetic criticism and to inquire into the meaning of that separation between common sense and specialist appraisal of individual poems which is so striking a feature of the contemporary literary situation. But it might be well first to try to frame some general definitions of prose and poetry and related terms. Having attempted to state a tenable point of view on these general questions, we shall then be in a position to discuss more particular aspects of the modern attitude.

Let us, then, begin by inquiring into the difference between poetry and prose. Both forms of expression use words as their medium, and the difference must lie largely in the way in which words are exploited by each. The poet uses the intellectual meaning of words, as the prose writer does, and he also uses their associations and suggestions, their sound and rhythm, and the musical and other patterns they form in combination with each other. But this is not enough to distinguish poetic from prose expression: a prose novel, too, will use aspects of language not employed in scientific prose—the sound and rhythm and "color" of words—only in less degree than the poet. Is the difference between poetic and prose expression, then, simply one of degree? Is it simply that in poetry the rhythm is more regular and the dependence on the suggestions, associations, and sound of words greater than in prose? And if this is so, where are we going to draw the line between the two kinds of expression?

Before trying to answer these questions, we might raise one more, the answer to which should lead to an answer to all the others. What is it in a poet's subject matter or in his way of apprehending his subject that makes him use language the way he does? This may sound a rather evasive way of posing the problem, for clearly we cannot tell much about the poet's way of apprehending his subject except through inquiring into the manner in which he has expressed it. But it is clear that if the expression is discerned by the experienced reader of poetry to be adequate, to be the inevitable expression for that particular subject matter, then there must be something either about the subject matter or about the poet's way of apprehending it that is essentially poetic, that makes poetic expression appropriate and inevitable. Again, however, we have the question: What is the subject matter apart from the poem? The history of poetry makes it clear enough that there is no natural poetic subject, that anything, if apprehended in the proper poetic way, can become the subject of poetry. So we cannot say that the difference between poetry and prose is that poetry, dealing with a poetic content, naturally finds a poetic form, while prose, dealing with a different kind of content, uses only the devices of expression appropriate to that art. As we have seen in discussing the genuine novel, there is no such simple mechanical relation between form and content in any art. But we can say that where there is poetic expression there must be a poetic way of apprehension in terms of which that kind of expression is the most complete and the most satisfactory (even the only possible), and the difference between prose and poetry is not simply a question of the degree to which certain aspects of language are employed: the difference between the two forms of literary expression lies primarily in the mode of apprehension in terms of which the kind of expression chosen becomes not only the best but the only adequate one.

It is thus the quality of insight which the poet brings to bear on his subject—or rather, out of which the subject matter arises—which makes the poetic method of expression necessary and inevitable. This is not to say that poetic insight can exist without poetry, for one of the main tests of poetic insight is that it must seek expression in poetry. And we can say that the insight of the poet differs from that of the prose artist just because of the different use of the medium of language to which each is driven. The poet employs all the denotational (referring to specific intellectual meaning), connotational (referring to less precise associated meanings), and emotional resources of language, but this in itself, as we have seen, would distinguish poetry in degree but not in kind from prose. A more significant differentiating factor in poetry is that the poet uses these aspects of language in such a way as to make some of them *comment on* the meaning and significance indicated by the other resources of words: this comment provides increased specification and particularization and at the same time, paradoxically, it provides new enlargement and enrichment—so that the significance of the whole is at once specified and universalized. Good poetry is the result of the adequate counterpointing of the different resources of words (meaning, associations, rhythm, music, order, and so forth) in establishing a total complex of significant expression.

A poem therefore is not distinguished from a work of

prose literature by the fact that, in giving expression to its meaning, it uses resources of language that are not employed by the writer of prose: it is distinguished from prose literature in that, whereas in prose the aspects of language employed reinforce each other as gestures emphasize speech, in poetry the aspects of language employed, being as a rule more various, are employed in a more complex and paradoxical way—one set of qualities providing instructions for interpreting the meaning that emerges from another set, not simply emphasizing, but modifying, specifying, enriching, reminding, disciplining, liberating, restraining, urging on—doing any or all of these things (even distorting and contradicting) in the service of the final totality of meaning. Poetry moves further away from prose and nearer "pure" poetry according as the different elements of the medium are used in counterpoint rather than in simply repeating the melody simultaneously an octave higher or lower. Thus to describe a dance in tripping words and in a dance rhythm is the simplest kind of poetic effect: in a great poem that effect would be enriched and complicated by all kinds of countersuggestions and expansions deriving from a subtle use of sound, suggestion, and association.

Consider, for example, these three stanzas by a minor eighteenth-century poetess:

> Methinks this world is oddly made,
>   And everything's amiss,
> A dull presuming atheist said,
> As stretched, he lay beneath a shade,
>   And instancéd in this:
>
> Behold, quoth he, that mighty thing,
>   A pumpkin, large and round,

Is held but by a little string,
Which upward cannot make it spring,
    Or bear it from the ground.

While on this oak a fruit so small,
    So disproportioned, grows,
That, who with sense surveys this All,
This universal, casual, ball,
    Its ill contrivance knows.

Here the use of those resources of language other than
simple denotation is limited to the reinforcing of the meaning by a simple but monotonous rhythm and a certain con-
trivance that keeps the sentences of a similar length and
pattern and provides a regular alternation of rhyme to
mark the end of each phrase. Put beside these three stanzas
another three in which the actual "content" is no more
profound but where the technique is much more complex:

It is an ancient Mariner,
And he stoppeth one of three.
'By thy long beard and glittering eye,
Now wherefore stopp'st thou me?

The bridegroom's doors are opened wide,
And I am next of kin;
The guests are met, the feast is set:
May'st hear the merry din.'

He holds him with his skinny hand,
'There was a ship,' quoth he.
'Hold off! unhand me, gray-beard loon!'
Eftsoon his hand dropt he.

Here we find, in the first place, that the rhythm, rhyme
scheme, and verse form do not simply serve to give neat-

ness or emphasis to each proposition made: they function in a much subtler manner. The contrast between the wedding guest's mood, expectant of secular celebration, and the new mood that is suddenly thrust on him by the stranger, is deliberately ignored by the placid flow of the simple stanzas, and as a result becomes all the more intense and mysterious, all the more effective as preparation for the strange story that is to follow. The deliberate introduction of the direct speech of each of the speakers without any break in the flow of the rhythm, the simplicity of statement suggesting an uncanny foreboding ("he stoppeth *one of three*"), the casual-seeming juxtaposition of the two worlds—the everyday and the unusual—the use of normal adjectives in a context which gives them an abnormal suggestion ("*skinny* hand"), the quiet dropping of an antique word in the midst of an almost colloquial diction (which nevertheless is not colloquial because of the use of the "thou" forms), the internal rhyme in the third line of the second stanza indicating a certain jollity and confidence that contrasts strangely with the foreboding suggested by images in the previous and succeeding stanzas—these are just some of the devices indicating that in this poem the poet is not using the resources of language in simple cumulation, but in counterpoint: Coleridge is not using any *more* of the resources of language than Lady Winchilsea (the author of the first three stanzas quoted), but he is using them in a more poetic manner. In both poems metrical and rhyme schemes are simple—they are actually simpler in the second—but it is the way in which rhythm and rhyme are counterpointed to the meaning put across by the other resources of language employed that distinguishes the poet from the accomplished versifier. Poetry is more than a series of propositions reinforced by regular metre and rhyme.

It should be added that the kinds of effect achieved by Coleridge in "The Ancient Mariner" can be achieved in prose fiction, but in prose fiction the nature and order of the actions presented play a more important part in creating the total effect than the counterpointing of the different aspects of language. Style, as we have seen, does at each point help to give the proper expansion of meaning to the plot in a genuine novel but it does so in a less oblique and complex manner than the "style" of poetry. To put the matter perhaps oversimply: in prose fiction the disposition of the action carries the greater load, while in poetry it is the use of the resources of language in relation to each other that bears the major burden. *Both aim at achieving the same kind of end.* The function and value of a poem and a piece of imaginative prose literature are the same: the means employed differ. Put the opening chapters of *Moby Dick* beside the opening stanzas of "The Ancient Mariner" and see how comparable effects (comparable but of course by no means identical) are achieved by very different ways of relating action to the use of language. Both build up an atmosphere of guilt and foreboding with reference to the sea, but Melville lets the actions—their nature and their order—set the main meanings going, while Coleridge relies initially on the counterpointing of different aspects of words.

Language as an art medium has both a formal and a representational aspect: like color and form in painting, it can stand for something in the world of experience but it can also possess a pattern independent of its representational significance. It is possible to figure out the *dialectic* of a poem—theoretically at least—regardless of its *meaning*. Unlike musical sound (which is rarely representational, and when it is, as in the cuckoo notes in the Pastoral Symphony, a deliberately unusual effect is intended) words represent things and say things at the same time. Thus the appreciation of music is both more difficult and more simple than that of poetry—more difficult in that there is no representational starting point or jumping-off place, as it were, to help the listener get started; and simpler, in that the composer has not to reckon with the listener's interest in the content rendering him insensitive to form. This latter danger is often present in painting and poetry. The work of art is *misread* through the reader's having an attitude to certain fragments of the meaning that prevents him from reading it as the aesthetic whole that it is. Further, in painting and poetry the representational aspect has a greater variety of possible degrees of importance, the extremes varying from "purely" abstract to "purely" representational art. Color and form may or may not have deliberate reference to anything that exists in the real world, while language, on the other hand, always has a meaning, a *denotatum*, so long as it is language and not mere sound, so that the distinction between abstract and representational art is in poetry a difference in tendency only. The problem as far as poetry is concerned is therefore this: How does the poet establish the representational aspects of his poem, how does he make clear to the reader the amount of relative credit he is to give to each of the different aspects of language as used in poetry? This problem does not exist in music, and it is less acute in painting, where the abstracting or universalizing of form is immediately visible to the eye. But in poetry it is very real. How is the reader to know whether the line "Child Rowland to the dark tower came" is the initial event in a series of related incidents whose aesthetic significance emerges from the nature of the plot pattern or is a purely lyrical statement to be understood as a symbol of romantic action? The answer can only be this: the difference must be made clear by adequate use of aspects of language other than the simple "denotational." These aspects must be exploited in such a way as to predispose the experienced and sensitive reader to the proper interpretation. The status of the wedding guest in Coleridge's "Ancient Mariner" is not made clear by the words considered simply in their representational capacity, but by the combined effect of all the aspects of words, poetically used. And if Coleridge had expressed his meaning in words considered simply as denotational or representational symbols and then reinforced that meaning by employing the sound and rhythm of the same words, he would have produced, instead of genuine poetry, that kind of emphatic rhetoric of which Macaulay provides some of the finest examples. This is not to say that Macaulay's verse is bad, but that the standard to be applied to it is not strictly a poetic one in this sense.

There is another kind of poetry which is really splendid rhetorical verse rather than poetry in the sense here defined, and one of the best examples of this is Johnson's "Vanity of Human Wishes." Here the sentiments are given added weight and cogency by the form in which they are expressed, the recurring pairs of rhymes hammering home the points, the regular metrical beat underlining relentless pictures of human greed or pride leading to disaster, the packed epigrammatic statement adding ironical force to the warnings and admonitions. The resources of language are not here used in a different way than they are in good prose, but they are used in a different degree.

It is a commonplace that in literary expression the place of any part of the statement in the total pattern of the whole is of more significance than it is in nonliterary statement. Poetry is that kind of literary statement which depends to the maximum degree on the order of the individual word, and that is because in employing the resources of language in the manner that has been indicated, the poet makes the order of words serve an extremely important function. Often he arranges the words in such an order that until the total complex of meaning is achieved no premature leakage of meaning can occur, and the poem remains obscure until, on a complete and careful reading, the meaning finally "explodes" (to use Gerard Manley Hopkins' term). This suspension of meaning until the total pattern is complete is only one of many means the poet may employ in order to make sure that the reader reads the poem in the proper way, reads it for what it is and not as a series of propositions simply. Rhyme and metre are, of course, the more obvious ways of safeguarding the poetic qualities of a poem (and they serve other functions, too) but this should not blind us to the fact that all kinds of delayed-action devices can be used with tremendous effect for the same purpose. Indeed, what is, say, the sonnet form but a device for keeping the reader from premature interpretation until the poem is complete? All, or nearly all, lyric poetry is obscure in the sense that the meaning does not progress in simple distinguishable stages but is kept partly hidden until the form has been completed. This is particularly true of poetry which does not use a specifically poetic diction, for when such a diction is used it is less necessary to safeguard against misreading, the diction alone being sufficient to warn the reader against any simple propositional interpretation. That is why poets whose diction is not specifically poetical —Donne, Rilke, Eliot—are more careful to guard against the escape of premature meanings by keeping the whole in suspense until the form is complete than poets like Spenser or Milton who can afford to be more propositional in structure because both their diction and their strict metre help to serve as reading instructions. Thus a poem which employs a poetic diction tends to show less "obscurity" than a poem which includes in its vocabulary everyday speech: when the poet does not compensate for this lack of a poetic diction by this kind of obscurity, then he runs the risk of falling into the trap into which Wordsworth fell in such a poem as "Simon Lee, the Old Huntsman":

> Few months of life has he in store
> As he to you will tell,
> For still, the more he works, the more
> Do his weak ankles swell.
> My gentle reader, I perceive
> How patiently you've waited,
> And now I fear that you expect
> Some tale will be related.

What is wrong here is not an "unpoetic" diction—for any kind of diction can be properly employed in poetry—but a complete lack of any devices to prevent the statements from becoming merely propositional.

If poetry at its richest and most mature demands what might be called, by analogy with music, the "contrapuntal" use of the different resources of language, it must nevertheless be admitted that in simpler and less profound kinds of poetry the "melodic line" of the poem often appears to be unenriched by any such complex use of the potentialities of words, sense being molded simply to the sound and rhythm. Robert Herrick provides many examples of poems of this kind:

> Cherry-ripe, ripe, ripe I cry,
> Full and fair ones; come and buy.
> If so be you ask me where
> They do grow, I answer: There,
> Where my Julia's lips do smile;
> There's the land, or cherry-isle,
> Whose plantations fully show
> All the year where cherries grow.

The poetic interest here appears to arise from the fact that the poet has taken an apt but rather obvious analogy and neatly wrapped it round eight lines, metrically equal and rhymed in pairs. We appreciate the deftness with which form and content have been wedded. Yet even here, by such devices as the shifting of the pause within the line so that it occurs in a different place in each line, and the setting of the actual rhythm—which is not strictly regular—against the regular metrical scheme which is nevertheless suggested, Herrick has achieved something more than a neat idea neatly expressed. Further, it will be noticed that the content falls into three parts: there is the statement, the anticipated question that arises from the statement, and then the answer. Thus, while the form is dual (eight lines, in couplets), the idea it expresses is triple. And this gives a new meaning to the whole. The poet arrests attention by a street cry ("Cherry-ripe!") expressed in a line which by itself is not poetic at all:

Cherry-ripe, ripe, ripe I cry.

In this line the basic metrical scheme is not yet set up, and the repetition of the high-pitched monosyllable "ripe" is compelling, but compelling like a shout rather than like a work of art. In the second line the pace is slowed down, the metre becomes evident, and the dramatic status of the author becomes apparent. When, in the third line, the poet moves into a hypothetical dialogue with a line consisting of equal monosyllables with no pause (or an equal pause) between them, the first line now becomes, in retrospect, poetic. The fourth line, building on this new discovery of the reader's, takes advantage of the suspense in the meaning provided by the ending of the third line in the midst of a dependent clause and prepares for the transition from the market place to the lover's bower (as it were) with especially effective pause (again, running *against* the metrical scheme and for that reason all the more striking; for the pause is on the rhyme word) at the actual moment of transition—the word "There" being the link between the two halves of the conceit, between the idea of cherries as fruit and as lips, just as a sustained note on a single instrument can bridge two sections of an orchestral work. The basic meaning of the poem derives from a simple contrast between the two interpretations of "cherry-ripe," yet as a dramatic poem it is triple in form; the author cries his cherries, his audience asks where they are, and he replies. There is thus a constant, and effective, tension between dual and triple form in the poem. There is also a tension—and tension in this sense might be defined as an apparent conflict of meanings which results in an enrichment of the total meaning—between the purely descriptive and the purely dramatic aspects of the poem. Slight as it is, the poem is nevertheless a "conceit" expressed partly dramatically and partly descriptively, having for its most obvious function the communication of a compliment and deriving poetic effectiveness largely from the tension between the dual and triple aspects of the poem as finally produced. In fact, even in this "simple" little lyric we have an example of the functioning of those laws of poetic expression already described.

Criticism could probe much further, and examine the exact significance of a word like "plantations" in this context, or dwell on the paradox of the poet's offering to sell to all comers cherries which turn out to be his Julia's lips. The lover who offers to sell his mistress's favors to the public is not paying her an unmixed compliment. The critic could inquire whether, in the reversal of the usual situation in which the lover is the slave of his mistress without openly rejecting the traditional position, the poet may not have achieved something quite different from a poem of simple compliment—a truly paradoxical poem whose total complex of meaning cannot be expressed in any paraphrase. Yet "Cherry Ripe" is, as poems go, a fairly simple lyric, and the fact that so many of Herrick's poems achieve their greatest effect as songs, set to music and sung, is testimony to their relative simplicity. The richest kinds of poetry—a sonnet of Shakespeare, a lyric of Milton, an ode of Keats—do not leave room for any further expressive device, just as no one would dream of setting words to a late Beethoven quartet. But to a simple dance tune one might well put words, and enhance rather than spoil the effect of the music.

Simplicity in poetry is obviously a relative matter, and the foregoing analysis of Herrick's "Cherry Ripe" will show that an apparent simplicity often conceals a cunning art.

Put a poem by Edgar Guest beside the simplest trifle by Herrick and it will be at once apparent that while both appear equally simple the former is inferior because it does not employ language poetically—it is just a commonplace idea expressed in rhyme and metre. But we should note that the most commonplace idea—such as the comparison between lips and cherries—if given adequate poetic expression ceases to be commonplace and takes on a new richness of meaning. And adequate poetic expression means much more than merely expression in rhymed and metrical lines.

What, then, about the ballad and the folk song? Here again it must be observed that the simplicity of such poems is very different from the simplicity of the commonplace modern versifier. Dr. Johnson's parody—

> I put my hat upon my head
> And walked into the Strand,
> And there I met another man
> Whose hat was in his hand—

misses the point because it misses this distinction. For folk poetry at its best is not the trite statement in verse of an obvious or silly situation: it is the endeavor to achieve adequate poetic expression of an emotional situation without the use of any references other than those suggested directly by experience. To limit oneself to such firsthand devices is to make poetic expression more difficult—for no help can be sought from literary allusion or from any other kind of direct association—but gives it a peculiar effectiveness once it has been achieved:

> Fowles in the frith,
> The fisses in the flod.

And I mon waxe wod; [1]
Mulch sorwe I walke with
For best of bon and blod.

This little early English lyric is difficult to match in any literature for sheer intensity of expression. Conscious or not, the art with which it is constructed is of the highest kind. First there is the reference in clearly articulated and unemotional lines to the contented life of the natural world; then, in one somber and striking line, the contrast between nature and the speaker; and finally, in the concluding two lines, the reason for this contrast. The variations in metre, counterpointed to the basic metrical scheme, correspond to and intensify the different elements in the content. The isolation of the third line—the pivot, as it were, of the poem —and the slowing down of the rhythm in the fourth line, beginning impressively with two funeral beats, combine with the helpless matter-of-factness of the concluding line to make the poem die away on an echoing plangent note. The poem is over before we realize it: the total meaning has been achieved with complete economy, and it reverberates in the mind. The poem, it will be noted, does not begin with a statement in the first person, but only moves into a personal statement in the third line; and this movement from descriptive to confessional utterance provides the element of paradox that enriches the total poetic significance. We have here more than versified propositions, for the propositions are arranged in such an order that the total meaning is different from the mere sum of the separate lines. This is what distinguishes it from Dr. Johnson's mock folk poem.[2] The distinction is even clearer if we put beside John-

---

[1] Wod: "mad."

[2] Dr. Johnson, when he composed this impromptu parody, was not

son's four lines one of the most famous quatrains in early
English poetry:

> Western wind, when wilt thou blow,
> The small rain down can rain?
> Christ, if my love were in my arms
> And I in my bed again!

It is not true, of course, that all folk poetry is good: much
of it is quite poor. But the kind of simplicity that character-
izes folk poetry is not necessarily the kind of simplicity that
makes for bad poetry, such as we find in "Simon Lee, the
Old Huntsman" or in the numerous parodies of Wordsworth, such as "The Baby's Début":

> My brother Jack was nine in May,
> And I was eight on New-year's-day;
> So in Kate Wilson's shop
> Papa (he's my papa and Jack's)
> Bought me, last week, a doll of wax,
> And brother Jack a top. . . .

In the latter case we have a trivial subject matter expressed
in a series of versified propositions, with no additional illumination provided by the manner of expression. The
typical folk poem takes an experience that has continually
impressed its significance on the minds of generations of
sensitive people and gives it poetic expression without going
beyond the limits of that experience in finding devices to
enrich the total meaning. It is this limitation of reference
that makes the folk poem, when it is successful, so impres-

---

in fact mocking folk poetry, but poking fun at a poem by Thomas
Percy entitled "The Hermit of Warkworth." Johnson was ridiculing
its stanza form. Later critics—including Wordsworth—have assumed
that he was parodying Percy's *Reliques*.

sive: such limitation constitutes "simplicity" only in a very special sense.

It need hardly be said that the poetic use of language can be found in many different degrees and put to a great variety of purposes. In the narrative poems of Sir Walter Scott (so little read now, but excellent stuff of their kind) the poetic use of language figures in a much less organic capacity than it does in a poem of Mallarmé or of Donne: poetic expression in *The Lady of the Lake* or *Marmion* is in a sense decorative in function: the main narrative line is determined by the simple propositional value of the sentences, but at intervals the resources of language are used poetically to amplify and enrich the meaning in a manner comparable to but by no means identical with the way in which incidental lyrics are used in Scott's novels. This is not to say that narrative poetry such as Scott wrote consists of versified narrative interspersed with lyrics, but it does mean that the central core of meaning, which is a narrative *continuum*, does not depend on purely poetic techniques for its expression, and poetic techniques function as a sort of commentary on this central core rather than as an organic part of it. This is also true, in some degree, of poetic drama, where poetic expression enriches but does not determine the main line of the action. Yet even this is to make too rigid a distinction, for in the greatest poetic drama the enrichment becomes an organic part of the meaning of the action, particularly when, as in Shakespeare's tragedies, the action is itself largely psychological in nature. Nevertheless even in Shakespeare the poetical effect is limited to the individual speech or passage; it is the poetic expression of a phase of the action, not, as in a Shakespeare sonnet, the total meaning of the whole work. In other words, poetic drama uses the poetic handling of language to express situations within the context of the play rather than to determine the general line of plot development. An adequate criticism of a poetic drama would therefore have to discuss the plot (in terms that would be equally appropriate to prose fiction) as well as the poetic technique employed to specify and enrich the meaning of the action at any given point. (It should of course be added that the critic of any drama would also have to concern himself with those aspects of the dramatist's presentation of his theme which constitute effective use of the medium of the theatre. The relation of the written to the acted drama could be the subject of a whole book by itself.)

The manner and degree in which the poetic use of language figures in a work of literature will depend on the scope and nature of the work. The lyric, which nineteenth-century critics generally regarded as the highest kind of poetry, differs from the long poem in that in it the pattern and significance of the whole is achieved by the simultaneous (or almost simultaneous) poetic use of all the resources of language, and the degree to which language is thus poetically used remains constant throughout the poem. This does not mean that the lyric must be placed above other kinds of poetry, for the most appropriate use of poetic expression—that is, its use in such a way as to provide maximum significance in the parts *and* the whole—in any kind of poetry will make it adequate and impressive as a work of art, and there seems to be no more reason for distinguishing, say, the lyric from the epic on the grounds that the former is "purer" poetry than for considering a short musical composition superior to a symphony. The most effective art is always that in which the resources of the medium are most adequately used with reference to the scope and scale of the work.

In any general discussion of poetry it is important to remember that it is the way and not simply the degree in which the resources of language are employed that differentiates the poetic handling of language as a literary medium from other kinds of handling. The use of sound effects, for example, to combine with other aspects of language in producing the total significance can vary tremendously from poem to poem. In such a poem as Wordsworth's "Lines Written in Early Spring" there is no emphasis on the purely musical quality of words in the obvious sense at all: sound, as an element in the meaning, is employed only in its rhythmic aspects, in the use of rhyme, and in the effective alternation of one- and two-syllabled words:

> I heard a thousand blended notes
>   While in a grove I sat reclined,
> In that sweet mood when pleasant thoughts
>   Bring sad thoughts to the mind.
>
> To her fair works did nature link
>   The human soul that through me ran;
> And much it grieved my heart to think
>   What man has made of man.

In the course of the six stanzas of this poem an idea, which is limited and defined through the intellectual meaning of the words used, is enriched and expanded into the expression of a mood in virtue not only of the "denotation" of the words but also of the complex of significance which emerges from effects of metre and rhyme, the selection and organization of images, and similar "poetic" devices. Use of the sheer musical sound of the words—their incantatory value—is hardly found in this poem at all. Put it beside, say, the "Ballat of Our Lady" by the late-fifteenth-century Scottish poet

William Dunbar, and it will be seen how poems can differ in the *degree* to which they employ incantation as a part of the poetic medium. (We deliberately choose a poem which will be unfamiliar and perhaps obscure to the American reader, for in such a situation the incantatory aspect of the language will strike him all the more forcefully.)

> Hale, sterne superne! Hale, in eterne,
>   In Godis sicht to schyne!
> Lucerne in derne for to discerne
>   Be glory and grace devyne;
> Hodiern, modern, sempitern,
>   Angelicall regyne!
> Our term inferne for to dispern
>   Helpe, rialest rosyne.
>   *Ave Maria, gracia plena!*
>   Haile, fresche floure femynyne!
> Yerne us, guberne, virgin matern,
>   Of reuth baith rute and ryne.

The solemn chiming that rings through this poem provides a single sustained emotional note against which the groups of short lines speak their meaning, and the total significance that results is expressible in terms neither of the sound nor of the sense, but only through both together. An example from another Scottish poet, Robert Burns, will show a use of sound midway between that of Wordsworth and Dunbar:

> O, my luve is like a red, red rose,
>   That's newly sprung in June.
> O, my luve is like the melodie
>   That's sweetly play'd in tune.
>
> As fair art thou, my bonnie lass,
>   So deep in luve am I,

And I will luve thee still, my dear,
  Till a' the seas gang dry.

Till a' the seas gang dry, my dear,
  And the rocks melt wi' the sun!
And I will love thee still, my dear,
  While the sands o' life shall run.

And fare thee weel, my only luve,
  And fare thee weel a while!
And I will come again, my luve,
  Tho it were ten thousand mile!

In Wordsworth's poem, the reader's first reaction is to the work in its propositional aspect, and this is modified and altered as the poem proceeds by the effect of metrical, imagistic, and other devices. In Dunbar's hymn the initial reaction of the reader is simply to the organ effect of the sound, and then this is both specified and enriched by the impinging on the musical background of the literal meaning of the words employed. In Burns's poem (deliberately kept at a simple level because it was meant to be sung) neither the propositional nor the melodic aspect of the expression strikes the reader first; the words are in themselves trivial and the metre is in itself commonplace; but propositions, imagery, analogies, metre, rhyme, and pattern together communicate simultaneously to the reader that note of passion with the undertone of melancholy, that mixture of recklessness and sadness, of tenderness and swagger, that distinguishes this, as a love *poem*, from a proposal or a confession. Yet all three poems use language poetically and are distinguished from nonpoetical literary expression in the peculiar combination of complexity and directness that marks their use of language rather than in any quantitative superiority in the number of aspects of language employed.

The difference between poetry and prose as a literary medium is thus not simply one of degree, though the difference between *verse* and prose *is* only one of degree. Verse can be good or bad on its own standard, without being judged as poetry at all. W. E. Aytoun produced some first-rate verse but cannot claim consideration as a poet. On the other hand, when Wordsworth fails as a poet he does not automatically become a good verse writer—as Scott often does when his poetic inspiration fails. The more conscious the poet is of the purely poetic aspects of language as a literary medium, the more likely he is to produce either good poetry or else something which is neither good poetry nor good verse. When Gerard Manley Hopkins fails he does not fall into competent pedestrian verse, nor does Donne: with such writers it is all or nothing—either the meaning "explodes" poetically, or it never achieves unity of meaning at all. A poet like Keats, when he fails, succeeds in writing indifferent poetry (not, like Scott, good verse; nor, like Hopkins, simply poetry that does not come off) because Keats's failures, most of which occur among his earliest writings, derive from an immaturity of taste existing side by side with an adequate poetic technique.

So far, more has been said about poetry than about poems, because we have been chiefly concerned with the way in which the poetic use of language in literature differs from the prose use. In discussing the way in which the resources of language are exploited in order to put across the total meaning, we find ourselves talking differently if we move from prose to poetry, but in discussing the kind of unity which a work of literary art possesses, the relation of form to content within such a work, and the kind of value which that work possesses, our conclusions will be the same for a poem as for a novel—provided, of course, that both are really literature. Poems, like novels, give to the experienced and sensitive reader that unique combination of insight and recognition which only art provides. The reader of poetry, like the reader of any effective work of imaginative literature, gets more than the pleasure of recognizing technical skill, more than the insight that derives from a new pattern's being imposed on an aspect of experience, more than the recognition of what he has in some sense known but never been able to express or to realize he knew until the moment of reading. It gives all these things. "I think," wrote Keats to John Taylor, "poetry should surprise with a fine excess and not by Singularity—it should strike the reader as a wording of his own highest thoughts, and appear almost a Remembrance." *Almost* a remembrance: for poetry, while letting us recognize what we knew, at the same time reminds us of what we had never known before. And if this is a paradox, it is because all art is in some sense a paradox, soothing and exciting simultaneously.

If the kind of pleasure afforded by the reading of poetry is more intense than that provided by prose, it is also true that poetry demands more active co-operation on the reader's part. That is why good poetic literature will never be as popular as good prose. A great novel has many levels of meaning which can in some degree be separated and appreciated each by itself. At least one can read a novel simply for the "story" and ignore all that richness of meaning which makes the story something more than "what happens next." But in poetry the different elements are so fused that one can rarely isolate a surface meaning and read the poem for that meaning alone. The appreciation of poetry demands both more effort and more experience in reading than the appreciation of prose. It is strange that this should be so, for poetry is in a sense a more primitive kind of art than prose and at one time in the history of every civilization was more universally used and appreciated. It is a measure of the degree of the artificiality of our civilization today that poetry should be a less popular and more difficult art than prose. The ordinary reader has quite lost that sensitivity to the poetic handling of language which, as was mentioned in Chapter I, a wholly illiterate population is likely to possess. Once again, we are paying the penalty of universal semi-literacy. Semiliteracy destroys the ability to appreciate poetry without giving the ability fully to appreciate prose. It produces a total insensitivity to all aspects of language except the coarsest representational aspects. It produces a taste for uniformity, for the catchword and the cliché, and an impatience with variety. And yet, underlying all this, there still exists in most people the primitive feeling for poetry, dulled, perhaps, and much weakened through lack of exercise, but not altogether dead. How to reach it and develop it is one of the great problems of modern education. All our education at present tends not to develop it but to drive it deeper and deeper into the limbo of lost faculties. Poetry in our schools is associated with explanatory notes of the most useless and pedantic kind and with every sort of ir-relevant encumbrance. If this is not changed soon, poetry may become a lost art. For "to have great poets there must be great audiences too."

II

The reader familiar with modern criticism of poetry will not need to be told that the emphasis on the element of paradox in poetic expression which he will have noted in the foregoing discussion is in keeping with the contemporary trend. The richness and most profound poems do seem to be those which employ the resources of language in some such manner, and it is one of the achievements of modern criticism to have recognized this. Yet it would be ridiculous to regard poetry as simply paradoxical statement. There is nothing valuable about the paradox itself; but the kind of counterpointing of different aspects of language which is employed by the fullest poetic expression—which is what gives poetry its element of paradox—does make possible a richer and more subtly organized form of statement, a form of statement, in fact, which can convey simultaneously several attitudes, all of which combine to communicate an insight, a complex sense of significance, which could not be communicated in any other way. But one cannot say that a poem is bad if it is not paradoxical or that it is good if it contains plenty of paradoxes. All one can say is that if a poem is successfully paradoxical in this sense, then the poet is using his medium in a more characteristically poetic manner than the writer of less paradoxical poems. But to use language in a less characteristically poetic manner is not necessarily to write a bad poem.

"A *Poem*," wrote Ben Jonson, "is the work of the Poet; the end and fruit of his labor and study. *Poesy* is his skill, or craft of making." This distinction between a poem and poesy is a helpful one, for it enables us to distinguish between the quality of a given poem and the kind of skill employed in writing it. Just as in prose narrative there is a continuous scale ranging from journalism to art, and works may fall anywhere in that scale, so there are different degrees in the poetic use of language, and one cannot simply say that the less the degree the worse the poem. Many contemporary poets, highly self-conscious about the place of paradox in poetic expression, make a deliberate effort to achieve a full poetic use of language, yet by their very self-consciousness and deliberateness fail to produce poems that are nearly as good as something written, say, by a good eighteenth-century poet whose use of language comes somewhere between the prose and the poetic use. Paradox, ambivalence, the simultaneous expression of different attitudes through the counterpointing of different aspects of language, will only succeed in a poem if properly put at the service of an insight, a sense of significance, that can use them. This is not to say that the poet must always start with that insight and then proceed to find a use of language that will communicate it—we are not concerned here with the psychology of creation; but it does mean that the poem should justify its use of language by what it says. A poem which does not justify its use of language by what it says is a bad poem, however "paradoxical" it may be. On the other hand, a poet who employs effectively a handling of language not at the highest point of the scale that extends from prose to poetry may produce a first-rate poem. Matthew Prior, the late seventeenth- and early eighteenth-century poet whom Saintsbury called (with justice) the first great English master of *vers de société* used language in a manner more characteristic of good verse than in the richest poetic way, yet he produced some of the most perfect things of their kind in English literature. How far up in the hierarchy of literary "kinds" one puts such poems is perhaps a matter of opinion; the point to be stressed here is simply that they are not inferior simply because they do not use language paradoxically.

Nor is the greatest poet the one whose use of language is most explicitly paradoxical, though many modern critics make the mistake of so believing. Donne is not at his greatest where his paradoxes obtrude themselves on the reader's notice. "Sweetest love, I do not go" is a better poem than "The Triple Fool." And Donne is nowhere as great a poet as Milton: "Lycidas," where the paradoxes are subdued and woven completely into the texture of the expression, is the finest nondramatic poem of the seventeenth century and one of the half-dozen finest in the English language. Critics who make use of a partial insight to introduce drastic new legislation on poetic taste are not doing a service to the understanding and appreciation of literature. Nothing is easier for a critic with any skill at analysis than to maintain that no poem can be good unless it is complex and paradoxical and then proceed to demonstrate the qualities of complexity and paradox in the poems he likes and to show their absence in those he dislikes. If Keats must be proved to be as paradoxical as Donne before he can be accepted, the task can be done with a little ingenuity; and it is not more difficult to explain the badness of Joyce Kilmer's "Trees" by demonstrating its total lack of paradox. But the ingenious application of a priori theories does not advance understanding. With sufficient ingenuity, anything can be proved either to possess or to lack complexity and paradox. If we wished to prove "Trees" to be a good poem on modern standards we could start with the change from the passive to the active voice in the last two lines—

> Poems are made by fools like me,
> But only God can make a tree—

and work this out as the climax of a most complex development of the theme of man the creator and the created and God as both simultaneously (the Spinozistic *natura naturans* and *natura naturata*); so that we could read the poem as a subtle commentary on the *De Intellectus Emendatione*. This would, of course, be ridiculous, for there is in fact no such subtlety in the poem. But who is to tell whether what the critic sees in the poem is "objectively" in it, once we depart from the mere surface meaning? What control can the ordinary reader have? These are not unanswerable questions, but they do suggest the nature of the problem. The analysis of any literary work to show its complexity is, for anyone reasonably intelligent and with some practice at that sort of thing, one of the easiest of all critical activities. One can always find complexity in advance if one wishes to find it, so that this kind of analysis can never *prove* a poem to be good but can only show how a critic who assumes beforehand that the poem in question is good can always prove it to be so to his own satisfaction if the criterion he uses is merely one of complexity, paradox, or some such quality.

The critic, therefore, must beware of postulating complexity or paradox *as such* as the criterion of poetic expression; for, in the first place, as such they have no necessary value and, in the second place, the degree to which these qualities objectively inhere in any given work is most difficult to ascertain. That these qualities play an important part in the most characteristically poetic use of the medium of language is—to repeat a point already made—one of the truths about poetry popularized by modern criticism. But the literary critic who, taking advantage of the revival of interest in the metaphysical poets of the seventeenth century, of the influence of Donne and Hopkins on modern poetry, and of the differentiating qualities of modern taste, tries to build these factors into a new normative view of what is good poetry and what is bad and bolsters this view by highly subjective analyses calculated to demonstrate these "modern" qualities in those poems which contemporary taste admires and show their absence in all others—such a critic is not fulfilling the critic's true function, which should surely be, not to implement changes in literary fashion with appropriate generalizations and particularities, but to rise above such changes in order to get a clearer and sounder view of the true nature of poetry. A practicing poet can be forgiven if his criticism is unduly narrow and fashionable, for he is engaged in working out a way of writing for himself and while doing so is bound to be in some degree unsympathetic to those working in some other tradition; but that is all the more reason for those critics who are not themselves poets to maintain their objectivity and integrity, and to relate the achievements of good contemporary poets to some profitable and broadly based generalizations about the nature of poetry in general. Creative writers can be expected either to create new fashions or to follow them, and we look to critics to explain and, where necessary, to popularize those fashions; but for the critic to be a slave of fashion is a betrayal of trust.

It may be argued that the alternative is a facile eclecticism; but that need not be so. The alternative is an appreciation of the richness and variety of imaginative literature, a recognition of the fact that the literary mind works in many ways and with many different materials, and, in the case of poetry, an awareness of the scale that runs from prose expression through verse to the most intense kind of poetic expression and of the fact that good literature can be achieved at any point in this scale. To censure Milton because he did not write like Donne, or Browning because he did not write like Hopkins, is no more sensible than to attack Dickens for not writing in verse. True, poetry is not a degree of prose any more than a symphony is a degree of a string quartet, but in each case there are effective ways of using the medium between the two. Unless we recognize this we shall be unable to discuss poems realistically, to give an account of poetry which is really relevant to what poets write and what readers read and enjoy.

It is not difficult to make the analysis of works of literature into a specialized skill which can be taught to disciples along with the appropriate terminology. This is now being done in many colleges. But how useful is such an activity? The gap between the experience of the ordinary educated reader and the pretentious analyses of the professional critics is already so great that serious criticism of poetry has ceased to serve any social function at all. Criticism of poetry has become to a large extent an exhibitionist exercise which gratifies the performer and impresses some of those academics who are trying not to be academics but which has no effect whatever on the reading public. The blame for this state of affairs does not lie wholly with modern critics—it is part of a split in modern culture which goes very deep, a symptom of a much more widespread disease—but the critics are not wholly guiltless. That pompous puritanism in the literary approach of so many of the more consciously "high-brow" contemporary critics has alienated many more than it has enlightened.

We quoted earlier a poem by Lady Winchilsea to show what may be called a very low-pressure use of poetic language: there was clearly no paradox there, no complex counterpointing of different aspects of language, but only a simple use of rhyme and metre for the purpose of making the expression of the thought neater and more regularly shaped. The defects of this poem, however, are not necessarily to be ascribed to this very limited use of the poetic medium, but rather to the jog-trotting roundabout manner in which the author proceeds to make her point: there is here neatness without economy. Almost any poem by Matthew Prior will show a not dissimilar use of the medium resulting in a much more successful poem. We might take, for example, the following:

Written in the Beginning of Mezeray's History of France

> Whate'er thy countrymen have done
> By law and wit, by sword and gun,
>   In thee is faithfully recited:
> And all the living world, that view
> Thy work, give thee the praises due,
>   At once instructed and delighted.
>
> Yet for the fame of all these deeds,
> What beggar in the Invalides,
>   With lameness broke, with blindness smitten,
> Wish'd ever decently to die,
> To have been either Mezeray,
>   Or any monarch he has written?
>
> It strange, dear author, yet it true is,
> That, down from Pharamond to Louis,
>   All covet life, yet call it pain:
> All feel the ill, yet shun the cure:
> Can sense this paradox endure?
>   Resolve me, Cambray, or Fontaine.

The man in graver tragic known
(Though his best part long since was done)
  Still on the stage desires to tarry:
And he who play'd the Harlequin,
After the jest still loads the scene
  Unwilling to retire, though weary.

It is not impossible to analyze this poem as though it were a poem by John Donne, but it would be unrealistic and unprofitable. The poet is here moving, through a series of quite simple propositions, from a contemplation of the history of France to a generalization about all men, and concludes by fixing the force of that generalization in our minds by an apposite image. The language in which this is expressed is rhymed and metrical, both rhyme and metre deftly managed in order to strike the ear helpfully—that is, the beat of the lines reinforces in a fairly simple manner the thought that each contains, while the chiming of the rhyme words helps to carry the reader on and fix the pattern of the expression in his mind. The slowing down of the final lines, where the image illustrates the movement from the impersonally philosophical to a more personal sense of *lacrimae rerum* (in which the whole poem, retrospectively, is anchored and from which it gets its elegiac note) is a perfectly simple but none the less effective device. It would be equally pedantic and silly to praise this poem for possessing the complexity and subtlety one could discover in a "metaphysical" poem or in an ode of Keats as to dismiss it for not possessing these qualities. This is, in fact, an excellent poem, though a poem which does not use language in the manner characteristic of the poetic medium at its richest and most distinctive (i.e., at its furthest remove from prose). The contemplation of such poems is as necessary for the critic (apart from adding to his enjoyment as a reader of poetry) as the analysis of profounder works, for it reminds him that there are many kinds of good poems and that a prematurely closed aesthetic system misleads more often than it illuminates. Is it old-fashioned or romantic (in the bad sense of the word) to claim that the critic's primary function should be to increase appreciation?

The analysis of poetry presented in the earlier part of this chapter is thus offered only as a partial view, a view of the most characteristically poetic kinds of poetry; but it might reasonably be maintained that any effective use of language in a work of literary art which differs from the way we employ language in ordinary prose discourse is a kind of poetry. Language is an art medium of many qualities and potentialities, and there are many ways in which it can be made to communicate that simultaneous combination of insight and recognition which is the characteristic of art. The names we give to this or that literary use of language are conventional and often quite arbitrary, and we are fooling ourselves if we imagine that definitions always advance understanding.

Poetry is not paradox, but it often uses paradox of a kind as part of the means to its end. Where it does so least obtrusively the poem is likely to be most successful—which is why we singled out "Lycidas" as a greater poem than anything by Donne, remarkable as many of Donne's poems are. In "Lycidas" we have a poem in which an enormous number of poetic devices are used to provide a constant expansion of the meaning, to make each statement include (one might almost say) its opposite; a poem in which each part is modified and enriched by its relation to other parts, each image takes on new meaning in the light of the preceding and succeeding images; a poem in which the whole achievement of Western civilization—classical and biblical, ancient and mediaeval and modern, pagan and Hebrew and Christian—is somehow embraced; which is both impersonal and personal, elegiac and exultant, derivative and original, topical and universal; yet it contains no shrieking paradoxes or obtrusive exercises of wit. It is a conventional pastoral elegy, and it closely follows the rules for that species of composition. Yet this single pastoral elegy, when read with care and understanding, will be seen to have for its subject a theme essentially the same as that of *Paradise Lost*—man's fate in the universe. For the theme of "Lycidas" is no less, unless perhaps we limit man to "man as poet," "man as genius"— the man of Renaissance humanism, in fact. "Lycidas," ostensibly a pastoral elegy written for the death of a friend, turns out to be a Christian humanist poem on man's fate.

These are large claims, and they cannot be fully substantiated in any short discussion; but we can at least attempt to indicate the grounds on which they are based. An analysis of "Lycidas" makes a fitting conclusion to any chapter on the nature of poetry.

The poem begins with a statement of the occasion which prompted it:

> Yet once more, O ye laurels, and once more
> Ye myrtles brown, with ivy never sere,
> I come to pluck your berries harsh and crude,
> And with forced fingers rude,
> Shatter your leaves before the mellowing year.
> Bitter constraint, and sad occasion dear,
> Compels me to disturb your season due:
> For Lycidas is dead, dead ere his prime,
> Young Lycidas, and hath not left his peer:
> Who would not sing for Lycidas? he knew

Himself to sing, and build the lofty rhyme.
He must not float upon his watery bier
Unwept, and welter to the parching wind,
Without the meed of some melodious tear.

The very first line introduces Milton in his capacity of young and ambitious poet: he is young because he has to pluck the berries of his art before they are ripe; he has already begun his career as a poet because this is not the first time he has plucked the unripe berries; and he thinks of himself (potentially at least) as a poet in the great classical tradition, as is made clear by his use of such images as laurel, myrtle, and ivy with their traditional associations with triumphant art. The berries may be unripe, but they are the true berries of art. He has to interrupt his period of apprenticeship, of self-dedication to learning his craft, to attempt a mature poem; he has to do so because the fate of a fellow poet compels him.

The note of compulsion is urgent. "Yet once more"—in these three opening words, three equally stressed monosyllables which take the reader into the poem suddenly and passionately yet which in themselves are very "ordinary" words with no obvious poetic qualities, we have the first hint of that strongly felt personal concern with himself and his own fate which is to be fully developed later in the poem. Yet that concern is not with his fate simply as man: it is with that aspect of himself which links him with the dead Lycidas and in the light of which Lycidas is himself an impressive subject—they are both poets.

Who would not sing for Lycidas? he knew
Himself to sing, and build the lofty rhyme.

The subject of the poem (as Tillyard and others have noted) is not Edward King, the drowned friend whom he laments under the name of Lycidas, but neither is it (as Tillyard claims) simply Milton himself. It is man in his creative capacity, man in his capacity for achieving something significant in his span on earth, man as Christian humanist. Lycidas has been drowned before he could fulfill his potentialities as a poet: man is always liable to be cut off before making his contribution; hence the lament, hence the problem, hence the poem. In "Lycidas" Milton circles round this problem, and with each circling he moves in nearer the center (he is spiraling rather than circling), and he reaches the center only when he has found a solution, or at least an attitude in terms of which the problem can be faced with equanimity.

There are many other points to be noted about these opening lines, and we shall select only a few. The image of the unripe berries and such phrases as "season due" and "mellowing year" introduce thus early in the poem the richly suggestive notion of the changing seasons with all the emotional implications of seedtime and harvest, of the death of the year being inevitably followed by its rebirth in the spring. These implications (which, it will be noted, convey a suggestion of comfort even while introducing the reason for lament) are not overstressed, but delicately handled by the rhymes and rhythms. The first sentence of the poem moves up to a climactic autumnal image:

> Shatter your leaves before the mellowing year

"Year" at the end of this line rhymes with "sere" (dry) at the end of the second line, and the two words echoing together form a contrast between the withered and the ripe, between death and hope. Thus not only is the theme fully presented in these opening lines, but there is also an antici- pation of the way in which it is going to be worked out. In the very run of this fifth and just-quoted line there is an implication both of action and of hope, the sharp gesture of "shatter" giving way to the image of "mellowing year" as the line slows down, so that the "forced" and "rude" fingers plucking the unripe berries almost become, for a brief mo- ment, harvesting images of active laborers gathering ripe fruit.

The young poet faces the premature death of the unful- filled fellow poet. His first reaction is to sing a lament for him:

> He must not float upon his watery bier
> Unwept, and welter to the parching wind,
> Without the meed of some melodious tear.

These three lines bring the first verse paragraph to an end, on a note which combines resignation with resolve. This quiet close of the introduction not only provides a perfect balance for this opening paragraph, which rests, as it were, on these three lines; it also holds a note of anticipation, and so draws the reader further into the poem.

The reader versed in the pastoral tradition will find much richer meanings in this first paragraph. Echoes of Theocritus, Virgil, and Spenser (to mention only three) link the poem to a serious tradition in Western literature and help to expand the subject into more than one man's lament for his friend. This use of the convention of the pastoral elegy also helps to make the poem more impersonal and hence more universal, helps to expand the theme into that general discussion of the fate of creative man which, as we have noted, is Milton's real subject.

It is with a deliberate awareness of the classical pastoral tradition that Milton begins the actual elegy in the second verse paragraph:

> Begin then, sisters of the sacred well . . .

He is invoking the muses with almost ironical deliberation. The second word "then," almost suggests that this is the thing to do, this is the proper routine, as though he were saying: "Very well then, since Lycidas is to be mourned for, let us mourn for him in the orthodox way and bring in the standard references to muses and so on." Those who know Theocritus will recognize an echo of a line in the first Idyll, and this emphasizes the suggestion of routine, of Milton doing his duty. But this is more than a conventional elegy, and its subject is more than Lycidas (or rather its subject is Lycidas rather than Edward King, for when he has given his dead friend a classical name, he has elevated him to the status of fellow poet and from there the expansion to creative man is inevitable). He does not stay long with these traditional statements, but, with a significantly short line, turns the subject to himself as poet:

> So may some gentle muse
> With lucky words favour my destined urn,
> And as he passes turn,
> And bid fair peace be to my sable shroud.

He will do this for Lycidas so that it will be done in turn for him: it is what is due to a poet. The death of Lycidas is now linked to the inevitable death of all men, however talented, however great their promise or achievements; even

the present celebrator will in his turn become the cele-
brated. There is a restrained note of self-pity here, conveyed
not so much by the actual words used as by the suggestion
given to the words by rhyme and metre. The short lines in
which he breaks off to draw the parallel with himself is
echoed by a later short line which is pure action or gesture
—a striking image of Milton's elegist turning to invoke
peace on *his* remains:

> And as he passes turn,
> And bid fair peace be to my sable shroud.

Nothing could better illustrate the importance of metrical
and semantic context in poetic expression than the first of
these two lines. In itself, it is a wholly "neutral" line, con-
taining no arresting word or phrase, no striking image. But
in its context the very simplicity of the expression, the
shortness of the line (echoing in length the other short
line two lines before, but rhyming with the immediately
preceding long line), and its effect purely as sound (three
light monosyllables followed by a leaning on the first syllable
of "passes" and then on "turn") combine with the purely
intellectual meaning to flash forth a significant and moving
gesture. Milton has now substituted himself for Lycidas in
the poem, but not before both men have been identified as
poets and so in a sense are identified with a larger and more
general conception of man. Having made the substitution,
he again points out why he has done it:

> For we were nursed upon the self-same hill,
> Fed the same flock, by fountain, shade, and rill.

This is a restatement of the earlier

> Who would not sing for Lycidas? he knew
> Himself to sing, and build the lofty rhyme,

but whereas the first time it had been an explanation of why he should sing for Lycidas, the second time it is an explanation of why both Lycidas and himself merit the same consideration. The reason in each case is the same: they are both poets. The description, in the following verse paragraph, is not so much (as the commentators would have it) an account in pastoral imagery of their life together as students in Cambridge; it is an account of their joint self-dedication as poets, and the pastoral imagery is employed in order to link their function as poets with the tradition of Western literature. This continuous linking of the theme with classical mythology is not decorative but functional: it keeps the poem rooted in an elevated conception of the nature, scope, and historical significance of the poet's art. It also helps to provide the proper "aesthetic distance" between the reader and the poem, maintaining a deliberate artificiality in the light of which the whole allegorical tone of "Lycidas" can be seen as adding universality and dignity to the subject.

One notes in this third paragraph a genuine emotion about nature which blends effectively with the purely conventional characteristics of the pastoral imagery and which reminds the reader of such earlier images as "mellowing year":

> Together both, ere the high lawns appeared
> Under the opening eyelids of the morn,
> We drove afield, and both together heard
> What time the gray-fly winds her sultry horn,
> Battening our flocks with the fresh dews of night,
> Oft till the star that rose, at evening, bright
> Toward heaven's descent had sloped his westering wheel.
> Meanwhile the rural ditties were not mute,

> Tempered to the oaten flute,
> Rough Satyrs danced, and Fauns with cloven heel,
> From the glad sound would not be absent long,
> And old Damoetas loved to hear our song.

In the first part of this paragraph we get a sense of community in an elemental activity. Such a phrase as "the opening eyelids of the morn" (a literal rendering of a Hebrew phrase used in the third chapter of Job, though also common in the Elizabethan poets) or "the star that rose at evening bright" introduces that favorite attitude to nature regarded with a sense of the passing of time already hinted at in the fifth line of the poem and to be used at the end of the poem in a single great phrase suggesting the dawn of a new day unobtrusively yet with immense promise:

> While the still morn went out with sandals gray.

One cannot help being reminded (though of course this is not relevant to a consideration of "Lycidas" itself) of that later moving outburst of the blind Milton at the opening of book three of *Paradise Lost:*

> Thus with the year
> Seasons return, but not to me returns
> Day, or the sweet approach of even or morn,
> Or sight the vernal bloom, or summer's rose,
> Or flocks, or herds, or human face divine.

The two poets are thus described pursuing their activities together against a background of changing nature, which culminates with the rising of the evening star, Hesperus:

> Oft with the star that rose, at evening, bright
> Toward heaven's descent had sloped his westering wheel.

And so our gaze is shifted from earth to heaven, and to a whole sense of cosmic implication, before the images suggesting poetry are introduced:

> Meanwhile the rural ditties were not mute,
> Tempered to the oaten flute. . . .

There is almost a suggestion of dance rhythms here, with the short line rhyming with the immediately preceding longer one. We do not need to speculate with the editors about the identity of "old Damoetas" in order to see in him a symbol of the approval of the properly constituted judges of poetry or at least of poetic ambition:

> And old Damoetas loved to hear our song

ends the paragraph on a note of self-satisfaction: they were both recognized as promising young poets. They pleased both those who judge merely by instinct (the rough satyrs and the fauns with cloven heel) and the cultivated critic. They were, in fact, both on their way to literary fame.

No sooner has he suggested this than Milton realizes afresh that one of them is no longer there, that poetic promise is not enough to guarantee immortality:

> But O the heavy change, now thou art gone,
> Now thou art gone, and never must return!

The images of nature which had previously suggested growth and maturity (i.e., change implying progress and hope) are replaced by nature images suggesting decay and death:

> Thee shepherd, thee the woods, and desert caves,
> With wild thyme and the gadding vine o'ergrown,
> And all their echoes mourn.

> The willows, and the hazel copses green,
> Shall now no more be seen,
> Fanning their joyous leaves to thy soft lays.
> As killing as the canker to the rose,
> Or taint-worm to the weanling herds that graze,
> Or frost to flowers, that their gay wardrobe wear,
> Where first the white-thorn blows;
> Such, Lycidas, thy loss to shepherd's ear.

One does not need to emphasize the emotional effect of such repetitions as "now thou art gone, now thou art gone, and never must return" or "thee shepherd, thee the woods . . ." or the sharpening of the meaning by the inversion in the latter of these. And here again it is Lycidas as poet who is mourned: it is the loss of his song, his loss to shepherd's *ear,* that matters. Even the songster cannot be saved—even the Muses cannot protect their own, as the succeeding verse paragraph immediately points out:

> Where were ye Nymphs when the remorseless deep
> Closed o'er the head of your loved Lycidas?

This is the second reference in the poem to the fact that Lycidas had met his death by drowning (as King in fact had been drowned), and it is introduced here in order that Milton may avail himself of appropriate mythological and topographical references. The water nymphs could not save him, nor could the tutelary spirits of that area near which the ship went down:

> For neither were ye playing on the steep,
> Where your old bards, the famous Druids lie,
> Nor on the shaggy top of Mona high,
> Nor yet where Deva spreads her wizard stream:
> Ay me, I fondly dream!

Had ye been there—for what could that have done?
What could the muse herself that Orpheus bore,
The muse herself, for her enchanting son
Whom universal nature did lament,
When by the rout that made the hideous roar,
His glory visage down the stream was sent,
Down the swift Hebrus to the Lesbian shore.

King had been drowned off the north coast of Wales, a fact which allows Milton to exploit the old Celtic traditions of Britain (since Wales became the repository of such traditions after the Anglo-Saxon invasions) and enrich the classical pastoral conception of the poet with references to the ancient Druids, especially associated with the island of Mona or Anglesey, and to the whole Celtic conception of the bard with its implications. "Deva" is the River Dee, which forms part of the boundary between England and Wales, and is rich is Celtic folk traditions (hence "wizard stream"). Milton has here deftly widened his conception of the poet to include both the classical and the Celtic; and to clinch this paragraph he returns to a classical image, picturing the frightful death of Orpheus, himself the son of Calliope, one of the Muses, and the very embodiment of poetic genius. Orpheus, the founder and symbol of poetry and a son of the Muses, could not be saved from a more frightful death than that which befell Lycidas; and Milton briefly but effectively touches on the gruesome story (told both by Virgil and by Ovid) of his being torn to pieces by the frenzied Thracian women, his head being cast into the River Hebrus and carried out to the island of Lesbos. The emotion reaches its height with that final, terrible image:

His gory visage down the stream was sent,
Down the swift Hebrus to the Lesbian shore.

The concept of the poet has by now been completely universalized; it is no longer Milton and his friend but the poet in both his classical and Celtic aspects; yet this is the fate he may expect. Why, then, he asks in the paragraph that follows, should one bother to dedicate oneself to a life of preparation for great poetry? This paragraph links itself at once to the third paragraph, which, as we have noted, describes such a life as led by Milton and his friend.

> Alas! What boots it with uncessant care
> To tend the homely slighted shepherd's trade
> And strictly meditate the thankless muse . . . ?

Is it worth trying to be a poet? One pursues fame, but before one has won it one is liable to be cut off. This is the theme of this well-known passage in which Milton effectively contrasts images of self-dedication with images of self-indulgence. Can man as Christian humanist achieve anything more than man as mere sensualist? This is one of the main questions posed by the poem, and its answer emerges implicitly only at the poem's end. For the moment, the poet finds a tentative answer, but it clearly does not satisfy him any more than it provides a satisfactory conclusion to the poem:

> Fame is no plant that grows on mortal soil,
> Nor in the glistering foil
> Set off to the world, nor in broad rumour lies,
> But lives and spreads aloft by those pure eyes,
> And perfect witness of all-judging Jove;
> As he pronounces lastly on each deed,
> Of so much fame in heaven expect thy meed.

This reply, given to the poet by Phoebus (Apollo, the god of song and music) is not convincing even in purely formal terms. An explicit reply of this kind would have to be given by a more inclusive representative of poetry than Apollo, for the poem includes nonclassical (e.g., Celtic and Christian) concepts of the poet as well. And the pat aphoristic nature of that final couplet—

> As he pronounces lastly on each deed,
> Of so much fame in heaven except thy meed—

could not possibly be the solution to such a complex poem as "Lycidas." There is almost a note of irony in the copybook lesson. It is a deliberately false climax, and Milton returns to his pastoral imagery to contemplate his theme again.

In the next verse paragraph Milton develops his earlier question— What were the responsible authorities doing to allow such a disaster to befall Lycidas?—in traditional pastoral style. This fact is itself sufficient indication that he is not satisfied with the solution he has just brought forward. The god of the sea, the god of the winds, and the Nereids, are each interrogated or considered, and each is cleared of having caused Lycidas' death. The poet has here given up for the moment any attempt at a larger solution to the whole problem posed by his friend's death and is trying to find out only who is immediately responsible. But he can find no answer to the question, except the baffling one that it was destiny:

> It was that fatal and perfidious bark
> Built in the eclipse, and rigged with curses dark,
> That sunk so low that sacred head of thine.

The section thus ends on a note of frustration and even despair. Dark images of superstition and fatalism provide the only response to his questions. This seventh verse paragraph, which moves from cheerful pastoral imagery to the suggestion of man's helplessness against fate, is worth careful consideration: in structure, movement, and balance it shows remarkable craftsmanship. We can pause only to note the sense of muttering frustration to which the poet is reduced at the end:

> That sunk so low that sacred head of thine.

But with the adjective "sacred" a new thought emerges: Lycidas, like Milton, had been a dedicated man—Edward King had, in fact, been destined for the Church, and thus was dedicated in a sense that Milton himself was not. His university could ill spare such a student, and the Church could ill spare such a recruit. The hero as poet is now enlarged to encompass the hero as Christian champion, and as such his loss is deplored both by Cambridge (represented by Camus, the River Cam) and Saint Peter. (It is worth noting that Milton uses biographical facts about King only where they help him to expand his meaning at the proper point in the poem; others he ignores or even distorts.)

The point now becomes not the loss to the poet by dying young and being unable to fulfill his potentialities, but the loss to society by having the poet (now expanded to mean spiritual leader as well as singer) die before he can serve it. And so we have the famous statement of Saint Peter:

> Last came, and last did go,
> The pilot of the Galilean lake,
> Two massy keys he bore of metals twain,
> (The golden opes, the iron shuts amain).
> He shook his mitered locks, and stern bespake,

"How well could I have spared for thee young swain,
Enow of such as for their bellies' sake,
Creep and intrude, and climb into the fold?
Of other care they little reckoning make,
Than how to scramble at the shearers' feast,
And shove away the worthy bidden guest.
Blind mouths! that scarce themselves know how to hold
A sheep-hook, or have learned aught else the least
That to the faithful herdman's art belongs!
What recks it them? What need they? They are sped;
And when they list, their lean and flashy songs
Grate on their scrannel pipes of wretched straw,
The hungry sheep look up, and are not fed,
But swoln with wind, and the rank mist they draw,
Rot inwardly, and foul contagion spread:
Besides what the grim wolf with privy paw
Daily devours apace, and nothing said,
But that two-handed engine at the door,
Stands ready to smite once, and smite no more.

This passage is, of course, an attack on the Anglican clergy, but it is not the digression that critics have generally assumed it to be. Milton has been developing the theme that the good are destroyed while the bad remain—a theme which in turn emerges from his earlier point that there is no sense in choosing a life of self-dedication to great art if the dedicated man is given no preferential treatment by fate over that accorded to mere sensualists and opportunists. Not only is the potential poet-priest no more likely to survive and fulfill his promise, he seems actually less likely to survive than the evil men who do harm to society where the poet-priest would have done good. Granted that the poet must take his chance of survival along with everybody else, is it fair to *society* to cut him off and let the drones and the parasites remain? The theme of "Lycidas" is the fate of the Christian humanist (or poet-priest) in all his aspects, both as individual and as social figure. He brings forward the social aspect of the theme in this verse paragraph, and concludes this section by affirming that those who abuse the confidence of society will in due course be taken care of—an affirmation which looks back to the earlier statement that the poet, however early cut off, will be judged and rewarded in heaven and looks forward to the later picture of Lycidas receiving his reward in the next world.

Even this bitter passage retains the pastoral imagery— for Lycidas is still the poet (though now priest as well) and the pastoral imagery makes clear that Milton is distinguishing between good and bad practitioners of the art that Milton and Lycidas had practiced together when together they had battened their "flocks with the fresh dews of night." The bad priests are described as producing "lean and flashy *songs*." (It is significant that for Milton, with his passionately held high ideal of the poet's function, the identity or at least similarity of the priestly and the poetic function was a natural idea; it certainly emerges through the imagery of "Lycidas.") As the poem proceeds, the more we see the third verse paragraph, in which Milton describes himself and his friend sharing the poet's dedicated life together, as central: it is this section which first fully develops the pastoral terms as referring to the poetic and moral (or Christian humanist) activities of both Milton and Lycidas, and it is in the light of this section that the passage about the bad priests must be read.

The technical devices employed in this paragraph to indicate the poet's contempt for those he is attacking have often been noted and scarcely need elaboration here. Here again we have the gesture, the clearly seen movement, presented in terms which associate it with an attitude of contempt:

> Creep and intrude and climb into the fold.

This is a very precise line, with three verbs each possessing an exact, different, but complementary meaning. One might note also the effect in their contexts of such phrases as "shove away," "scramble," and "swollen with wind." These images, without ceasing to be precisely pastoral, immediately take the reader realistically into the situation Milton is attacking. One need hardly catalogue the effective qualities of such lines as:

> What recks it them? What need they? They are sped;
> And when they list, their lean and flashy songs
> Grate on their scrannel pipes of wretched straw.

By combining biblical with pastoral imagery (and of course biblical imagery is itself often pastoral, thus providing Milton with a handy link between the classical and the biblical, the pagan and the Christian) Milton brings his conception of poet and priest, of poet and moral leader, into closer association, so that lines like

> Of other care they little reckoning make,
> Than how to scramble at the shearers' feast,
> And shove away the worthy bidden guest,

with their reference to the parable in the twenty-second chapter of Matthew, provide imagery that is not merely decorative but functional. And the conclusion of this verse paragraph suggests, with deliberate and effective vagueness, that something will be done about those who abuse society's trust:

> But that two-handed engine at the door,
> Stands ready to smite once, and smite no more.

There is no need to follow the editors in their manifold speculations on what Milton really meant by the "two-handed engine": all that is necessary for an understanding of the poem is to note that retribution is certain through a device—"that two-handed engine"—which suggests purposive activity on the part of society. The implication of "two-handed" is that men will use it, use it with their two hands, and this suggestion of purposive activity anticipates and prepares the way for the final resolution of the problem posed by the poem—which is that man as poet and moralist should, so long as he remains alive, keep on working and striving, should continue to proceed from task to task until he is no longer able. Thus though the poem opens on a note of regret that the poet is forced once again to produce a poem before his talent is mature, it ends by his turning with renewed zeal to renewed poetic activity:

> Tomorrow to fresh woods and pastures new.

Having suggested the lines on which the resolution of the poem is to be achieved, Milton returns to the dead Lycidas, aware of the fact that the only answer to the problem posed by his premature death is for those who survive to carry on more zealously than ever. Such an answer implies an abandonment of sorrow and a leaving behind of thoughts of the dead potential poet, and before he can bring himself to do that he must try to transmute the dead Lycidas into something beautiful and fragrant. And so, as a sort of apology to

Lycidas before leaving him forever, he turns passionately to his dead body and attempts to smother it with flowers:

> Bring the rathe primrose that forsaken dies,
> The tufted crow-toe, and pale jessamine,
> The white pink, and the pansy freaked with jet,
> The glowing violet.
> The musk-rose, and the well-attired woodbine,
> With cowslips wan that hang the pensive head,
> And every flower that sad embroidery wears:
> Bring amaranthus all his beauty shed,
> And daffodillies fill their cups with tears,
> To strew the laureate hearse where Lycid lies.

It is a sort of amends to Lycidas for having to forsake him at the last, yet he is reluctant to do so:

> Ay me! Whilst thee the shores, and sounding seas
> Wash far away, where'er thy bones are hurled,
> Whether beyond the stormy Hebrides
> Where thou perhaps under the whelming tide
> Visitest the bottom of the monstrous world,
> Or whether thou to our moist vows denied,
> Sleepest by the fable of Bellerus old,
> Where the great vision of the guarded mount
> Looks toward Namancos and Bayona's hold;
> Look homeward angel now, and melt with ruth.
> And, O ye dolphins, waft the hapless youth.

The body of the dead Lycidas refuses to be smothered with flowers, refuses to allow the poet to "interpose a little ease" and "dally with false surmise." He is indeed drowned—but no sooner has Milton accepted this fact anew than, with a deliberate echo of the references to Mona and Deva in the fifth verse paragraph, he exploits geography with tremendous effect. Lycidas lies drowned off the coast of Wales.

Perhaps his body has been washed northwards up to the romantic Hebrides; perhaps he is exploring the monstrous depths of the ocean; perhaps—and here the emotion rises— he has made his peace with the great Celtic guardians of pre-Anglo-Saxon Britain (Celtic Britain always had an immense fascination for Milton) and sleeps with "the fable of Bellerus old," i.e., with the fabled Cornish giant whose name Milton constructed from the Latin name for Land's End, Bellerium. Milton here projects a sudden image of the whole southwest of England (Wales and Cornwall, with their sense of the Celtic heritage of Britain) and infuses into this projection a passionate sense of English history and English patriotism. The "guarded mount" is St. Michael's Mount, near Penzance. Following the possible drifting of Lycidas' body, Milton is led to associate it with that part of England, so rich in history and folklore, which projects into the sea and looks toward Spain (Namancos and Bayona's hold were districts in northern Spain, so marked in several seventeenth-century maps). England looking toward Spain suggests the whole challenge of Anglo-Spanish relations of the late sixteenth century, culminating in the defeat of the Spanish Armada in 1588. (Catholic Spain remained the enemy for the very Protestant Milton, and this passage has its links with the earlier reference to the "grim wolf with privy paw," which refers to the proselytizing Catholic Church.) To see Lycidas in this context is to see him in conjunction with English history and with the guardian angel of England, St. Michael, who looks out over the sea toward the long since defeated Spanish enemy. He has thus at last managed to associate the dead Lycidas with a sense of triumph, and he can now afford to leave the dead for a moment and interpose a great cry for the living:

> Look homeward angel now, and melt with ruth.
> And, O ye dolphins, waft the hapless youth.

Let St. Michael cease looking out to the long-defeated enemy, and take care of his own. Though on the surface this refers to his protecting the dead body of Lycidas, no careful reader can escape the feeling that Milton is pleading with St. Michael to look at the state of England, to cease looking out to sea but to examine conditions at home—and in so doing to see the role the young Milton has set for himself, and to help him to attain it. Look homeward at Lycidas— and at me, the poet seems to be saying. The dolphins can take care of the dead man; the living poet requires your active aid.

Whether we accept this refining of the meaning or not, we cannot fail to note a great surge of passion in that line—

> Look homeward angel now, and melt with ruth—

and Milton is only passionate in this poem when dealing with the problems and duties of the living poet, not with the fate of the dead one.

Lycidas can now be disposed of conventionally. The problem has moved beyond him, so Milton can let himself picture his reception in Heaven with all the triumphant resources of Christian imagery. And that is the function of the penultimate verse paragraph beginning:

> Weep no more, woeful shepherds weep no more.

There is a content here, a restrained passion, a controlled happiness. Milton has prepared the way for the emergence of the attitude in the light of which the question posed by the poem can be answered— What shall the Christian humanist do in the face of imminent death, what shall man the creator do in the prospect of extinction?—and having done so he can at last accept the conventional Christian answer to the question of Lycidas' own fate. The note of acquiescence emerges clearly here, as it did not in the answer provided earlier by Phoebus.

But this cannot be the end of the poem (as it should have been if the conventional interpretation of "Lycidas" were the right one). He has to return to himself, to man as poet and creator, and give his final statement on the question posed by the poem. What shall the creator do when he knows that he may die at any time? The answer, already prepared for in several passages, emerges at the end firmly and with conviction. We return to Milton, to the poet who has been mourning his dead friend. And as we return to him, a new day dawns, and he sets out on new tasks. The answer is not dissimilar to that given in the sonnets on his twenty-third birthday and on his blindness: man can only do what in him lies as best he can.

> Thus sang the uncouth swain to the oaks and rills,
> While the still morn went out with sandals gray,
> He touched the tender stops of various quills,
> With eager thought warbling his Doric lay:
> And now the sun had stretched out all the hills,
> And now was dropped into the western bay;
> At last he rose, and twitched his mantle blue:
> Tomorrow to fresh woods, and pastures new.

He returns at the end to those pastoral images most suggestive of the poet. He pays his respects to the Greek pastoral poets ("*Doric* lay") and to the Latin (the fifth line, as Verity and others have noted, is Virgil's *Majoresque cadunt altis de montibus umbrae*") and thus associates himself firmly with the Western literary tradition. And the last line suggests a determination to proceed to yet greater poetic achievements. Lycidas is forgotten; the world remains in the hands of the living and is shaped by their purposes.

This analysis is, of course, anything but complete. It would be possible to analyze in detail the function at each point of subtle metrical variations, of the various shapes of the different verse paragraphs, and of the differing line lengths and rhyme arrangements. There is in fact no limit to what the critic can say about a really successful poem. But perhaps enough has been suggested to indicate the immense richness of expression possible to the poetic medium. Whether we recognize all that has been drawn out of the poem as something really there or feel that some of it lies in the mind of the critic rather than in the poem itself, the fact remains that all this and much more can be suggested by "Lycidas." There is a complexity of expression in a good poem which cannot be achieved in any other kind of discourse, and an elaborate *explication de texte* can only suggest partially and awkwardly the kind of thing the poem is conveying much more subtly and immediately: it can never tell all that is in the poem, but it can help to indicate what the reader may find if he reads with his eyes open. Any good poem is much greater than the fullest paraphrase, for the poem achieves through simultaneous utterance a kind of expression which could keep the paraphrasing critics going endlessly.

As a footnote to "Lycidas," one might observe that the solution here presented by Milton is in a sense a very "classical" one: man faces the possibility of sudden death by determining to carry on, to proceed in the full utilization of his faculties as long as he is spared to do so. We see this equally, as we have already observed, in Milton's sonnet on his blindness, which need only be set beside Keats's sonnet "When I have fears that I may cease to be" to show how completely differently two poets can handle a similar situation. Here is Milton, the classical Christian humanist:

> When I consider how my light is spent,
>   Ere half my days, in this dark world and wide,
>   And that one talent which is death to hide,
>   Lodged with me useless, though my soul more bent
> To serve therewith my Maker, and present
>   My true account, lest he returning chide,
>   "Doth God exact day-labour, light denied,"
>   I fondly ask; but patience to prevent
> That murmur, soon replies, "God doth not need
>   Either man's work or his own gifts; who best
>   Bear his mild yoke, they serve him best; his state
> Is kingly. Thousands at his bidding speed
>   And post o'er land and ocean without rest:
>   They also serve who only stand and wait."

And here is Keats, "romantic" and sensitive, solving his problem by losing himself in a mood of infinite contemplation:

> When I have fears that I may cease to be
> Before my pen has gleaned my teeming brain,
> Before high-piléd books, in charactery,
> Hold like rich garners the full-ripened grain;
> When I behold upon the night's starred face
> Huge cloudy symbols of a high romance,
> And think that I may never live to trace
> Their shadows with the magic hand of chance;
> And when I feel, fair creature of an hour,
> That I shall never look upon thee more,

Never have relish in the fairy power
Of unreflecting love—then on the shore
Of the wide world I stand alone, and think
Till love and fame to nothingness do sink.

This is the problem of "Lycidas" posed and answered
equally poetically; but no two poems could be more unlike
in mood, texture, or technique.

‡ CHAPTER VIII ‡

Some Potentialities of Verse

MATTHEW ARNOLD, one of the least eccentric of English critics, refused to allow any poet in the category of the great classics unless his work possessed the quality of "high seriousness." Such a quality is difficult to demonstrate, for its discovery is a rather more subjective matter than the recognition of most literary qualities; we can, however, agree that a great work of literature must be ultimately serious in its implications however unserious it may be on the surface. (Arnold's failure to distinguish between explicit and implicit seriousness led him to undervalue Chaucer and Burns.) But neither the ordinary reader nor the professional critic spends more than a small fraction of his time reading the greatest classics; there are important minor kinds of writing which possess value and give pleasure which it would be unrealistic to ignore and pedantic to exclude from a discussion of literature. We have already noted some of these minor kinds of prose narrative. They are even more numerous, and often more interesting, in verse. Verse, so apt a form for the epigram or the mere exercise of wit or display of humor, offers possibilities for the skillful amateur more obvious than prose. There is a lot to be said for a training in verse writing as part of a liberal education: it helps to cultivate the ear, exercises the mind and, in some degree, the imagination, and adds to the number of personal and social pleasures. It also provides the apt amateur with a skill easier to acquire than its prose equivalent.

Verse is a more formal medium than prose. It offers a tighter discipline and therefore one within which the accomplished craftsman can operate with more confidence. (We are not, of course, talking of poetry, but merely of verse as a medium of expression and of the trained versifier.) In most civilizations there has been a greater "mob of gentlemen who wrote with ease" in verse than in prose. This is not as surprising as it may seem: any English schoolboy who has been trained to write Latin hexameters knows that once he has learned the rules he can turn out "correct" (if anything but inspired) Latin verse with much greater confidence than he can write Latin prose. And in one's own language it is easier for the trained practitioner to be witty, humorous, neat, or epigrammatic in verse than in prose. Verse is, in fact, the ideal medium for "light" literature.

The reading and writing of light verse for simple amusement is, however, possible only where there exists sufficient experience of literature to provide a sensitivity to different types of skill. Most light verse is a kind of implicit parody, which can only be fully appreciated by those who can appreciate what is being implicitly parodied. Nevertheless, the sheer wit of, say, Ogden Nash can be enjoyed even by those who do not read his poems as concealed parodies of kinds of serious poetry. It should be made clear at this stage that any suggestion that parody of serious poetry can only be enjoyed by those who do not enjoy serious poetry and therefore like to see it made fun of is wholly unjustified. The truth is the exact opposite. The best parodies are those which pick out and exaggerate certain characteristics of an author's style, and that isolation and exaggeration can only be adequately seen by those who can see that it *is* isolation and exaggeration. Of course, there is a kind of parody which is a fairly direct criticism of bad poetry. It consists merely in overdoing the faults of the original until they are obvious to everybody. But the subtlest and best kind of parody is that which depends on our appreciation of the good qualities in what is being parodied and whose effectiveness consists in the way in which those qualities, taken out of their context and used for different ends than those for which they are used in the original, present the "high-brow" masquerading as the philistine.

One of the most remarkable and cheering things about the appreciation of literature is that, in addition to the great and unique pleasures which it affords, to the enrichment of experience which it makes possible, it also makes possible so many other secondary pleasures. Every serious reader possesses what George Orwell has called in another connection an "unofficial self," which takes pleasure in laughing at those very things which, in his most serious and exalted moods, he so passionately admires. Just as only the believer can enjoy the luxury of blasphemy, so only the genuine lover of literature can enjoy fooling with the literary medium. The only essential quality he demands of such fooling is that it should be witty or at least clever. Verse gives an almost unlimited scope for the exercise of mere wit or cleverness (and it must be remembered that genuine nonsense is a form of wit). One can talk purer and more brilliant nonsense in verse than in prose, as Edward

Lear has proved, and one can also be more offensive, more incisive, and more mocking.

This is not to maintain, that all great literature consistently sounds a high serious note while literature that is not greatly but merely "good" uses similar techniques in a less serious way. As we have noted, literature can fulfill the high functions we have claimed for it without being obviously concerned with a profound and serious theme in a profound and serious way: there are comic and ironic insights which are just as illuminating and exciting as those afforded by tragedy. Cervantes is as great a writer as Racine, and Donne's love poetry is better than Elizabeth Barrett Browning's. As W. H. Auden and John Garrett put in their introduction to *The Poet's Tongue:* "A great many people dislike the idea of poetry as they dislike over-earnest people, because they imagine it is always worrying about the eternal verities." Great literature has always some relation, however indirect, to the "eternal verities," but it certainly does not *worry* about them. The colloquial shock of the opening of Donne's "The Canonization" rules out any obvious high seriousness of approach, but no love poem could be more serious in its implications:

> For Godsake hold your tongue, and let me love,
>   Or chide my palsie, or my gout,
> My five gray haires, or ruin'd fortune flout,
>   With wealth your state, your minde with Arts improve,
>   Take you a course, get you a place,
>   Observe his honour, or his grace,
> Or the Kings reall, or his stamped face
>   Contemplate, what you will, approve,
>   So you will let me love. . . .

When we talk of the minor pleasures of verse, therefore, we are not drawing a line between an obvious seriousness and an obvious lack of it: the distinction is between that kind of poetry in which form and content, inseparable and growing out of each other, provide a cumulative or explosive illumination, and the manipulation of verse expression in order to say something that is not otherwise inexpressible, but which is more agreeable or witty or emphatic if expressed in verse, or perhaps in order to say nothing at all while seeming to be saying something very significant, or in order to produce mimicry or parody.

It is an odd paradox that the less experience of literature a reader has, the more he demands an obvious seriousness in any kind of writing before he will respect it. A great deal of popular literature pretends to be a serious treatment of profound issues while in fact it is not, and, on the other hand, much great literature which is not widely read makes no such pretense while in fact having genuinely profound implications. The experienced reader has therefore two advantages over the semiliterate: he can realize the greatness of literature which is not obviously serious, and he can appreciate genuinely nonserious writing such as parody, nonsense verse, and craftily expressed triviality. The semiliterate is ashamed of his unofficial self and is afraid to enjoy it, while the really literate man has the means of making his unofficial self acceptable through wit or mockery and, deriving pleasure from sheer play with the literary medium, contemplates it with relish and without self-reproach.

Thus literature has its suburbs to which only those who know their way back to town have access. There are in addition doubtful places, partly in the suburbs and partly in town, which some would claim wholly for one and some wholly for the other. Some critics have seen an infinite sadness, an underlying tragic implication, behind the amusing nonsense of "The Dong with a Luminous Nose," while others see only elements of parody and self-mockery.

When awful darkness and silence reign
Over the great Gromboolian plain,
   Through the long, long wintry nights;—
   When the angry breakers roar
   As they beat on the rocky shore;—
When Storm-clouds brood on the towering heights
   Of the Hills of the Chankly Bore;—

Then, through the vast and gloomy dark,
There moves what seems a fiery spark,
   A lonely spark with silvery rays
      Piercing the coal-black night,—
   A meteor strange and bright:—
Hither and thither the vision strays,
      A single lurid light.

Slowly it wanders,—pauses,—creeps,—
Anon it sparkles,—flashes and leaps;
And ever as onward it gleaming goes
A light on the Bong-tree stems it throws.
And those who watch at that midnight hour
From Hall or Terrace, or lofty Tower,
Cry, as the wild light passes along,—
      "The Dong!—the Dong!
   "The wandering Dong through the forest goes!
      "The Dong! the Dong!
   "The Dong with a luminous Nose!"

This is a more amusing poem to those who have read Poe (one among several poets suggested by the opening) than to those who have not. It is not necessarily a parody of Poe's poetry, but the opening stanza, for example, is an attempt to build up an atmosphere of mystery which is seen to be comic when put beside genuine attempts of that kind, such as we find in Poe. "The Dong with a Luminous Nose" might be construed as a tragic poem if there were not other poems in the background with reference to which it is seen to be purely comic. And yet there is a strange, haunting quality—almost but never quite emancipated from implied reference to more clearly genuine examples of the kind—in the refrain:

> Far and few, far and few,
> Are the lands where the Jumblies live;
> Their heads are green, and their hands are blue,
> And they went to sea in a sieve.

This represents one kind of poetic resource (imagery made more memorable by sound), but that one kind is used in isolation, not as an organic part of a richer whole. Thus one kind of amusing light verse can be verse which uses only one kind of poetic resource while pretending that it is using them all. The poetry is only comic, however, if the pretense is not genuine but is itself pretended. If Lear in writing "The Dong with a Luminous Nose" had really believed that he was writing great tragic poetry he would probably have produced, not good comic verse, but simply very bad poetry.

Partial use of the poet's resources, employing one kind of device and making it do the work of all the others, can result in good comic or light verse if it is done deliberately, the poet being fully conscious that he is presenting the part as the whole; but if it is not done with such awareness on the part of the poet it results in bad poetry, or at least in serious poetry which has obvious faults. Many of Swinburne's poems have faults of this nature, and even in his best work there is always a tendency to promote rhythmic and imagistic devices to the supreme and even sole place in poetic expression.

> The ivy falls with the Bacchanal's hair
>   Over her eyebrows hiding her eyes;
> The wild vine slipping down leaves bare
>   Her bright breast shortening into sighs;
> The wild vine slips with the weight of its leaves,
>   But the buried ivy catches and cleaves
> To the limbs that glitter, the feet that scare
>   The wolf that follows, the fawn that flies.

Poetry that is too easily parodied is itself dangerously near parody. Swinburne was worlds away from Edward Lear in attitude and intention, but the disturbing truth is that the two poets remind us of each other. If a parody reminds us of a great poem, that is no reflection on the great poem; but if a poem intended to be great reminds us of a parody, then something is wrong.

The pleasures of minor verse therefore include the perception of implicit parody (and parody itself is implicit criticism, though not always valid criticism) in poems which to the inexperienced reader may be simply funny or simply silly or simply serious. The pleasures of open, professed parody are perhaps more obvious than those we derive from the implicit parody of certain kinds of comic verse, but they are not any more lively. Pure parody is fairly common in English literature, and the "purer" it is the more limited its effect. In the poetry of Edward Lear there is an indirect and subtle mimicry of any number of poets.

But in William Maginn's parody of Coleridge's "Ancient Mariner" we see only a reference to that particular poem, and as a result the verse soon loses its savor:

> It is an auncient Waggonere,
>   And hee stoppeth one of nine:—
> 'Now wherefore dost thou grip me soe
>   With that horny fist of thine?'

> 'The bridegroom's doors are opened wide,
>   And thither I must walke;
> Soe, by your leave, I must be gone,
>   I have no time for talke!'

To a reader who did not know what was being parodied, these verses would appear merely silly. The best kind of parody hits at its victim and *en route,* as it were, strikes other targets as well. Lewis Carroll's "You are old, Father William" is enjoyed by multitudes of people who do not realize that it is a parody of Southey: there is a ludicrous seriousness about it which is humorous in its own right. And it is humorous because it is an implicit parody of more than Southey: it strikes at all kinds of pretentious commonplace in literature and even at whatever can be made to appear pretentious commonplace if read in the wrong way. The kind of parody which can reduce its original at one blow to sheer nonsense can remain amusing for its nonsense even for those who do not appreciate the poem which the parody has annihilated. Such annihilation at one blow is not common, and again it is Lewis Carroll who provides the best examples. His parodies of Isaac Watts are wholly devastating because they do not bother to criticize by implication any phase of Watts' style or any favorite theme, but by altering the imagery reduce the whole thing instantly to unadulterated rubbish:

> How doth the little crocodile
> Improve his shining tail,
> And pour the waters of the Nile
> On every golden scale!

But in spite of this annihilation of Watts, the reader who has never heard of "How doth the little busy bee" can enjoy the poem because the application of rhyme and metre to sheer nonsense is itself funny. Carroll did the same thing to "Twinkle, twinkle, little star" with

> Twinkle, twinkle, little bat!
> How I wonder what you're at!
> Up above the world you fly,
> Like a tea-tray in the sky.

You appear to be following the same path as your original; you set out along it solemnly and conscientiously, and arrive promptly in Bedlam.

It should be emphasized that we can enjoy a parody while not admitting that there are any real faults in the poem which is being parodied. Yet there are certain kinds of poetry that are almost invulnerable to parody, and when the parodist aims at them it is often himself that he makes ridiculous rather than the object of his parody. There has probably never been a wholly successful parody of Shakespeare, and those that are even partly successful either refer to Shakespeare's earlier style or take passages so well known and so often quoted that the parody becomes rather an implicit criticism of those who continually quote the passages than criticism of the original. One can, of course (and it has been done), write a word-for-word parody of such a speech as "All the world's a stage" by changing the images all the way through, but that is not so much a parody of the poetry as of the ideas expressed in the poetry. Or one could write a parody of one of the more set speeches in *A Midsummer Night's Dream* by depressing all the images, but the result would not be the same as Lewis Carroll's parodies of Watts because Carroll is aiming at more than the images—he is out to get that kind of poetry. We can see this by putting such a speech beside such a parody.

> That very time I saw—but thou couldst not—
> Flying between the cold moon and the earth,
> Cupid all armed: a certain aim he took
> At a fair vestal, thronéd by the west,
> And loosed his love-shaft smartly from his bow,
> As it should pierce a hundred thousand hearts;
> But I might see young Cupid's fiery shaft
> Quenched in the chaste beams of the wat'ry moon:
> And the imperial Vot'ress passéd on,
> In maiden meditation, fancy free.

Put beside this Phoebe Cary's parody of it, and we see how limited an effect such a parody has:

> That very time I saw (but thou couldst not)
> Walking between the garden and the barn,
> Reuben, all armed; a certain aim he took
> At a young chicken, standing by a post,
> And loosed his bullet smartly from his gun,
> As he would kill a hundred thousand hens.
> But I might see young Reuben's fiery shot
> Lodged in the chaste board of the garden fence,
> And the domesticated fowl passed on,
> In henly meditation, bullet free.

This is amusing, in a mild way; but we only smile briefly. The reason for the difficulty of writing good parodies of Shakespeare is, perhaps, that there is no *general* Shakespearean style or attitude that we can aim at. We must, therefore, aim at specific passages and at specific words in them, and this kind of "pure" parody, as we have seen, is less effective than the kind which has more general reference.

Appreciation of parody and of the kind of light verse in which some degree of parody is implied is thus one of the many minor pleasures which a knowledge and appreciation of literature make possible. Parody is not, of course, confined to verse any more than exhibitions of deft and cunning craftsmanship for its own sake are confined to verse; but the formal requirements of verse make these kinds of activities more likely to be found in verse than in prose.

It is true, however, that while bad prose can never give pleasure, there is a kind of pleasure to be derived from thoroughly bad poetry. The spectacle of a would-be poet, filled with a high serious purpose and wholly unconscious of his total inability to handle the poetic medium, perpetrating verses full of every kind of technical horror—inept images, broken-backed versification, continual anticlimax, figures of speech that are ludicrous when they are meant to be elevating—is, under certain conditions, an amusing one. And the more appreciative of good poetry we are, the more amusing we shall find such stuff. It is a kind of poetry which is a running parody of itself. It must be wholly and irrevocably bad before we can take pleasure in it, for as long as any sign of grace remains we find the faults painful rather than funny. But there is a sublimity in total badness which only the lover of good literature can appreciate. "The Execution of Alice Holt" (which is included in the *Oxford Book of Light Verse*) is an example of this kind of verse:

> A dreadful case of murder,
> Such as we seldom hear,
> Committed was at Stockport,
> In the county of Cheshire.
> Where a mother, named Mary Bailey,
> They did so cruelly slaughter,
> By poison administered all in her beer,
> By her own daughter.

This is not perhaps the purest kind of bad poetry, for it has something of the quality of the doggerel street ballad, a kind of verse which is not the product of a man wholly incapable of writing poetry producing what he thinks are great poems but rather of a popular desire to have a convenient and easily memorized record of an event which has stirred the public imagination. Further, the last two lines of the stanza—

> By poison administered all in her beer,
> By her own daughter—

have something of a dying fall (produced largely by the short final line), which has a smack of poetry about it. A purer example of impressive badness is provided by the work of William McGonagall, the Scottish "bard" of the last century. His ode on the attempted assassination of Queen Victoria is a remarkable piece:

> God prosper long our noble Queen,
>   And long may she reign!
> Maclean he tried to shoot her,
>   But it was all in vain.

> For God he turned the ball aside,
>   Maclean aimed at her head,
> And he felt very angry
>   Because he didn't shoot her dead.

> Shakespeare says there's a divinity that hedgeth a king,
>   And so it does seem,
> And my opinion is, it has hedged
>   Our most gracious Queen. . . .

Or consider this perfect unconscious parody:

> Stately mansion of Baldovan,
> Most beautiful to see,
> Belonging to Sir John Ogilvy,
> Ex-M.P. for Dundee.

That stanza unconsciously creates the model which it is unwittingly parodying. The same is true of the remarkable "Battle of El-Teb":

> Ye sons of Britain, I think no shame
> To write in praise of brave General Graham,
> Whose name will be handed down to posterity without any
>   stigma
> Because, at the battle of El-Teb, he defeated Osman Digna.

And perhaps the most perfect couplet of all:

> Oh, wonderful city of Glasgow, with your triple expansion
>   engines,
> At the making of which your workmen get many singeins. . . .

The pleasure of enjoying pure badness in literature is reserved for those who know goodness and can thus recognize at once the kind of writing which is so wholly bad that no question of applying standards to it ever arises and which can be appreciated without afterthoughts as mag-

nificent rubbish. Where the badness is not quite so outrageous, the verse can be much more corrupting; for people
are likely to derive a standard for good poetry from sloppy
or stereotyped verse, which sounds like the real thing to the
inexperienced ear. The inexperienced ear will not be fooled
by McGonagall into setting him up as a standard, though
it may not recognize how far below all possible standards
he is.

The enjoyment of utter badness cannot be rated high
among the minor pleasures of verse, for the kind of stuff
that McGonagall wrote very quickly palls. Once we have
read a few examples we have had enough. But perhaps sufficient has been said to suggest that the medium of poetry,
even when it is not used to produce great poems, can be
played with in a great variety of ways very agreeably. Appreciation of these minor uses of verse is not, however, independent of appreciation of its major use. The more experienced and sensitive a reader is, the more he will delight,
in moments of relaxation, in writing which is simply witty
or simply craftsmanlike or simply funny. And he will have
provided for himself many new sources of humor, for what
is "simply funny" to him will often derive from implicit
parody and some kind of amusing disproportion, which can
only be seen as disproportion by those who know proportion. Every art has its host of subsidiary skills which derive
from it and which can be practiced and appreciated only
by those who appreciate the true art, and it also makes possible a kind of utter badness in which the connoisseur, recognizing for once a situation where he can throw all his
standards to the winds, can take unrestrained if short-lived
delight.

The moral is that if we learn to take literature seriously

we find a whole group of nonserious pleasures also open to us. Only the semiliterate is haunted by the thought that he ought always to be edified by what he reads. The literate reader is not always reading Shakespeare's tragedies or Dante's *Divine Comedy*. If we agree with Saintsbury that in the house of poetry there are many mansions, we should add that access to the greatest of them gives access to all.

‡ CHAPTER IX ‡

Literature and Belief

ONE ASPECT of the relation between *Dichtung* and *Wahrheit,* between imaginative literature and literal truth, continues to trouble the critics—indeed, it troubles them today perhaps more than it ever has. What is to be our attitude toward a poet whose beliefs differ radically from ours, who is working in a tradition which for us is invalid or meaningless? Can we really enjoy Dante if we are shocked by the idea that errors of faith deserve an eternity of punishment? Can we fully appreciate *Paradise Lost* if we feel that it has not in fact justified the ways of God to men? Or, to put the problem in a more typically modern form, can we appreciate the poems of Ezra Pound if he was a fascist? What are we to do with the fantastic mystical systems of Yeats? At what point, in short, does our disagreement with a writer's ideas interfere with our appreciation of his work as imaginative literature? Does what a poet believes *matter?*

If literary value consisted merely in the patterning of ideas or images or both, such questions could be easily dismissed. We could say at once that content is irrelevant and that all that matters is the way in which that content is arranged. And in a sense this would be true, for literary quality emerges from the way in which a work is ordered, not from any paraphrasable content. But, as we have emphasized, such an ordering serves a purpose; it does not exist for its own sake, though it is often possible to appreciate it for its own sake. Literature is that ordering of the expression which expands the meaning to the point where it produces cumulatively the maximum amount of insight into man's fate. But few works of literature are ostensibly written to serve such a purely literary purpose; many great writers, in fact, would refuse to recognize such a purpose as valid. And in any case all works of literature bear the marks of their author's beliefs and of the tradition in which he wrote. Often the proper significance of an image or an incident can only be appreciated with reference to those beliefs. Must we believe in marriage as an institution before we can accept the marriage of the hero and heroine at the end of a Shakespearean comedy or a Victorian novel as a satisfactory resolution of the plot? If the full expansion of meaning can often occur only with reference to the context of beliefs within which the writer operated, what happens when that context is shattered and the reader approaches the work without its assistance?

There are several points involved here. Insofar as the images, references, allusions, symbols employed by a writer derive their significance, either wholly or in part, from a particular context of beliefs and attitudes, knowledge of that context becomes as important for the reader as knowledge of the language in which the work is written—and it is important in the same kind of way. We cannot even see the "bare text" for what it is unless we have some knowledge of the cultural framework with reference to which the words have their full meaning. But this does not mean that we must agree with the beliefs shared by those who operated within that framework, any more than when we understand the word "civil" in its modern sense of "polite" we have to agree with its etymological implication that politeness is a necessary characteristic of citizens. We must know what gives meaning to expressions without necessarily agreeing with the beliefs which originally gave them that meaning. This is an aspect of all language and presents no very great problem. In works of imaginative literature (and especially in poetry), where meanings are made to reverberate into ever wider implications, we must know the frames of reference which enable the writer to achieve those reverberations, or remain with only a partial knowledge of his language. Some frames of reference are historical, and can be learned by study; others, however, depend on less objective factors and can be understood only through continued experience in reading. A poet uses language with reference to what men believe, what men know, and how men feel. Beliefs and knowledge change, and though the basic pattern in human emotions seems to have remained fairly stable throughout recorded history, there are minor variations even there.

It is not therefore a simple matter to see the work of literature in itself as it really is. We have to learn our poet's language, through developing an awareness of and a sensitivity to the kinds of richness of implication which he utilizes. It is not enough to say, particularly in dealing with a work of the past, that the reader must take the work as he finds it and that by looking at it simply as a self-existent poem or play or piece of fiction he can adequately appreciate it. This would be as logical as to say that a reader ignorant of Greek could take an ode of Pindar as he finds it and appreciate it as a collection of meaningless marks on paper. For the only completely objective existence a work of literature possesses is as a series of marks on paper. So-called "ontological" criticism can never really be practiced, and those who consider that their critical method is onto-logical are deceiving themselves. To understand a work of literature we must know the meaning of the text, but we cannot know that meaning fully unless we appreciate that it lies in the relation of what is written to what certain men have thought, felt, and known.

One need not share a writer's beliefs, therefore, before appreciating how they operate in enriching the meaning of the words he employs, but sometimes it is necessary to be aware of them. (It is not necessary to be aware of them when the reader unconsciously shares them: when Burns compares his love to a red rose we do not require any in-formation about Burns's attitude to redness and to roses, for in the experience of most men the two words stand for beauty and freshness in nature. This illustrates how the purely semantic aspect of words shades imperceptibly into the meanings they acquire from particular beliefs.) The same situation arises in larger units of plot. Marriage of hero and heroine as a symbol of the resolution of the action can be accepted even by readers who do not believe that marriage provides a stable and satisfactory relationship if in terms of the working out of the plot such a solution be-comes a symbol of such a relationship. If we did not know what marriage was, or if we never knew that men had at a certain period of civilization regarded it as the only satis-factory relationship between a man and a woman who loved each other, we would require some background informa-tion before we could fully understand and appreciate the ending of the story. With that information, if the work were well constructed, we should be in a position to appreciate the resolution of the plot whatever our personal beliefs about the relation between the sexes.

There would, however, be certain exceptions to this. A reader who felt violently that the whole idea of marriage involved a complete distortion of the facts of human nature, that marriage was essentially something false, ugly, and dishonest, would perhaps find himself unable to accept the ending as satisfactory however adequate the construction and however much information he had acquired about the beliefs of the author and of the society in which he moved. In situations of this kind it must be admitted that a reader's differences of belief from those of the author would affect his appreciation. Such situations do occur, and most readers have individual blind spots or sensitive areas which prevent them from understanding or appreciating certain works. Of course, a novel which is not a genuine work of imaginative literature but simply a fable designed to advocate a certain attitude or course of action will always fail to appeal to readers whose beliefs differ radically from those of the author. But this is a quite different problem. The interesting question concerns those who, whatever their intentions, have produced works of literature in the fullest sense.

But what are we to do when the very fabric of the work is constructed out of beliefs which we may repudiate? The answer to this question is not really as complicated as it may seem. All great works of literature contain more than their ostensible subject: starting from a particular set of beliefs, a story such as the biblical story of the temptation of Adam and Eve or a journey through the underworld, the true poet, in presenting his material, keeps reaching out at every point to touch aspects of the human situation which are real and recognizable whatever our beliefs may be. By turns of phrase, imagery, the simultaneous use of the musical and the semantic aspects of words, the deft ordering of words and events, the poet turns his story and his creed into a technical device for shedding light on man. The combined knowledge of man's nobility and his weaknesses, the sense of man's looking back or forward to a golden age coupled with the knowledge that, partly because of the very characteristics of man as man, such a golden age can only be envisioned but never realized, the sense that man's life is governed by change and linked always with the movements of the day to night and back to day, with the passing of the seasons, with resolutions that fluctuate and moods that alter, but a sense, too, that only a determination to do what can be done at the moment of decision can ever get man anywhere—all this and a thousand more such archetypical ideas are carried alive and passionately into the mind of the reader by Milton's *Paradise Lost;* and this is achieved, not in the pallid discursive way represented by the description just given, but implicitly, cumulatively, insistently, as the work flowers before the reader's eyes. We may feel that the debate in Heaven represents bad metaphysics and that God is in fact responsible for Satan and his activities; but though this attitude would be contrary to what Milton intended us to believe, he does not rest on his belief, for he has carried the meaning of his work infinitely further, so that, if as a theological work *Paradise Lost* is inadequate, as a *poem* it is completely adequate. As a poem its subject is not the justification of the ways of God to men but the essential and tragic ambiguity of the human animal. Expanding his meaning, by means of images, similes, and sheer choice of vocabulary, to include all that Western man had thought and felt, pivoting the action on a scene which, as Milton describes it in the poem, illuminates immediately the paradox of man's ambition (at once good because noble and bad because arrogant) and human love (both bad because selfish and because passion clouds the judgment and good because unselfish and self-sacrificing), linking the grandiose action at every point to images suggestive of man in his daily elemental activities in fields, cities, and on the ocean, developing, as in his picture of ideal nature in the early scenes in Eden, all the implications of man's perennial desire for a better world with the continuous awareness of man's tendency to trip himself up and turn his very virtues into snares—achieving all this in spite of the plot, as it were, by placing an image where it will sing most eloquently and by linking each unit to others so that the chorus of implication grows ever richer, reverberates ever more widely, Milton, by operating as a poet rather than as a theologian and moralist, in spite of himself probes deeper into man's fate than his formal scheme would seem to allow and in the magnificent close sums up in one climactic image all that has ever been said about man's capacity to hope in spite of despair, about loneliness and companionship, about the healing effects of time and the possibility of combining bewilderment with a sense of purpose, giving us, in fact, his final echoing statement about man's place in the world:

> Some natural tears they dropped, but wiped them soon;
> The world was all before them, where to choose
> Their place of rest, and Providence their guide:
> They hand in hand with wandering steps and slow,
> Through Eden took their solitary way.

That final couplet, read in the light of all the previous action, is Milton's last word on man, and, read in its context, it reaches out far beyond any agreement or disagreement with his conception of God's justice or man's responsibility for his fall. We see now that Milton's theological purpose and plot were, in a sense, as much a part of his *technique* as his language, and that the modern reader can regard them in that light.

Some modern critics have tried to make Dante and Milton acceptable to us by arguing that their literal beliefs are not absurd and can—and indeed should—be held by modern man. But this is to make appreciation of imaginative literature dependent on one's literal acceptance of the author's creed, and it is a dangerous activity for a literary critic. What are we to do with the Greek dramatists, with Lucretius and Virgil and innumerable other earlier writers, if we have to make their theology acceptable before we can justify them? A critic is, of course, perfectly free to defend Dante's or Milton's theology, but in doing so he is not acting in his capacity of literary critic. Moreover, it can be argued with some plausibility that the reader who is in literal agreement with such a writer as Dante or Milton or Bunyan is apt to interpret what he reads too narrowly and see it as a much less comprehensive and exciting work than it is in the eyes of the reader who comes to the author in order to read a work of imaginative literature. The history of Dante criticism, or of the criticism of any religious poet, tends to confirm the view that *literary* appreciation not only does not depend on complete agreement with the author's beliefs but often does not fully develop until the question of agreement or disagreement has been ruled out as irrelevant.

It is only possible, however, to consider an author's beliefs as part of his language or his technique when he does in fact use them as such—that is, when he is a poet (in the widest sense of the term) and uses his material poetically. If he does not use his material poetically, then the question of the rightness or wrongness of his framework of beliefs will be very relevant, for the value of the work will be as a contribution to ethical theory or religious thought or some similar category.

There are also occasions where a writer's beliefs are so narrow or corrupting or so at variance with anything that civilized man can tolerate that it becomes impossible to regard them as merely part of his technique. However, an interesting natural law of genius comes into operation here: if a man holds such narrow or corrupting beliefs, he will not in fact be able to handle them poetically, he will not be able to use his material in such a way that it becomes recognizable as an illumination of human experience. Technique must have something to base itself on, and as far as beliefs go, they may be right or wrong but they must be capable of leading the reader to man as he is, of reflecting genuine light on the human situation. A wholly preposterous view of man would, from a purely technical point of view, be incapable of being used poetically. This is not to say, of course, that every reasonable view of man can always be employed poetically, but it *is* true that a wholly ridiculous or corrupt view can never be so used.

This brings up the much debated question of art and fascism. Can a fascist (using the term to denote an attitude toward man and his destiny wholly abhorrent to civilized and thoughtful people) be a good artist? The first answer to this question would be on the lines of the preceding paragraph. A corrupt view of man can never be an adequate basis for art. (One must distinguish between a corrupt view and a wrong view: the former is always the latter, but the latter is not necessarily the former.) But there are occasions when people have, through ignorance or naïveté or self-deception, associated themselves with movements which discerning observers know to be the deliberate creation of corrupt minds, yet do not themselves share in that corruption. Political ignorance or naïveté will not necessarily prevent a writer from producing some kinds of effective literature. A poet could write a good imagist poem whatever his political or moral confusion. The degree to which such confusion would show itself in his art would depend on the scope of his art. Mere craftsmanship is independent of all beliefs, but, as we have seen, art is more than mere craftsmanship. Ezra Pound supported Italian fascism because he was confused and self-deceived, not because he was corrupt and malicious. His early poems, limited in scope and confining themselves largely to carefully etched pictures of individual scenes or situations, are excellent of their kind; his *Cantos* are confused and inartistic because in them he was attempting to do more than present specific images or perceptions, and the same self-deception and confusion which led him to support Italian fascism rendered him incapable of writing a coherent or significant long poem.

Literature of any scope can never be independent of beliefs, for the devices the writer uses in order to expand the implications of his statements until they achieve that continuously reverberating significance that is one of the marks of successful art depend at every point on the relation between object, situation, or incident and the place

they hold in human attitudes and creeds. When attitudes
and creeds change, that relation will change, and the reader
will have to recapture that attitude artificially if he wishes
to appreciate the work fully. When literature is produced
in an age which, like the present, has no common background of belief with reference to which objects, situations,
and incidents can be given literary meaning by the writer,
a problem arises of which every artist is all too aware.
Poets—for whom this problem is particularly acute—are
driven to try to create their own body of beliefs and present it (as Yeats did) to their readers as guides to the understanding of their works; or they are led to depend on purely
private associations or personal reading, which has led to
so much obscurity in modern poetry. The more able and
sensitive the poet, the more he will be driven to try to
find some sort of solution to this problem, by a private
mystical system, as in Yeats; by dependence on a personal
reading list, as Eliot did in *The Waste Land;* by autobiographical devices whose significance cannot be fully
known to the reader, as in some of the early poems of
Auden; or by other methods. It is a fault in poetry to be
obscure to contemporaries (to be obscure is not the same
as to be difficult, which is sometimes a virtue), but the
better the poet the more likely he is to have that fault
today. For the modern poet has, in fact, no contemporaries,
in the sense that Virgil or Dante or Milton or even Tennyson had: he cannot speak to men living under the same
curtain of beliefs for in our time such a curtain has almost
disappeared; he can speak with reference only to his own
personal universe. If we have to reconstruct the world of
Milton in order to appreciate fully the significance of each
phrase and image of *Paradise Lost* (though that poem is

intelligible and fascinating without *full* appreciation), we have no less to reconstruct the world of Eliot in order to appreciate fully the significance of each phrase and image in *The Waste Land*. And Milton's world he shared with his age; Eliot's is his own. Clearly a poet loses something by treating his contemporaries as posterity; it leads him to combine autobiographical with pontifical gestures, and they do not sort well together. Only Yeats, who knew how to season his personal symbolism with irony and sometimes with pure play, could, at his best, avoid the modern dilemma. This is not to say that there are no good modern poets or poems; but too few of them can be judged by the reader without preparation. We should not have to do that kind of homework in order to enjoy the work of our contemporaries; that we often have to do so is the fault not of the poet but of his age.

It would be an oversimplification to say that all good poets must today be obscure: certain kinds of poetry are less dependent on the poet's relation to a community of belief and can therefore be produced effectively whatever the state of public attitudes. But the fullest use of the characteristically poetic method demands the achievement of an expansion of meaning possible only when each unit of expression is set within a context of belief from which it derives continuous enrichment. Public belief becomes a matter of technique, and when it ceases to exist writers have often to find new technical devices to compensate for the loss of a device no longer available. To convey the individual sensibility of the writer directly and impressively to the reader, without first referring it to common notions which link reader and writer and in terms of which the meaning can be objectified and universalized, demands new

kinds of subtlety in expression, which we find in, for example, the novels of Virginia Woolf. The reason for the
great spate of technical experimentation and innovation
in both poetry and prose in the last fifty years is precisely
that the writers have been looking for ways of compensating by new technical devices for the loss of public belief.
Public belief is an aspect of language, and when it fails
language loses a dimension.

II

If the literary artist uses public belief as part of his
technique, it means that often the results are apparent in
his work without our having to reconstruct those beliefs
for ourselves. That is one reason why, even though a complete appreciation of all the implications of a past work
may demand some scholarship, great works of the past can
nevertheless generally be understood and enjoyed with
such preparation. The appreciation of past literature is,
indeed, often easier than the proper appraisal of contemporary writing. It is easy to see the value of books which
have been winnowed by time and which the diverse voices
of succeeding generations have acclaimed as great. Knowing that they must be great, we actively look for their impressive qualities and in doing so train ourselves to read
them. The judging of contemporary literature is much
more difficult. There is no unanimous voice of the generations to tell us which are good, no long array of critics to
point us to their virtues. We must make up our own minds.
And it is not always easy to assess the value of new works,
for it sometimes means dissociating ourselves from our
contemporary feelings about the situations described and

looking at the work as a whole as an effective artistic illumination of experience. The situations must be considered aesthetically, according to how they are integrated into a rich and significant pattern. But ultimately aesthetic significance is a human significance, a way of presenting insights into the human situation, so that there is no simple and mechanical means of divorcing one's attitude as contemporary human being from one's attitude as reader of a work of art. A situation might have tragic implications in view of what we know and feel about it today without those implications really deriving from anything in the book as written, and in such a case we might consider the book an effective tragedy because of our inability to see that those implications exist only for us in the circumstances in which we find ourselves and are not really effectively brought out in the book. We all make mistakes in judging contemporary literature; the most "objective" critic is not immune. It is perhaps easiest to go astray in poetry, for in the adequate reading of poetry we must actively give so much of ourselves that we are always in danger of giving too much, of contributing to the poem an emotional experience which derives solely from our own autobiography and for which there is no real warrant in the poem. The more experience we have of reading great works of literature, the more likely we shall be to avoid such mistakes, but in appraising new works we shall always make some. This may be why some critics prefer to confine their reading to older literature; but that is the coward's way out. We do no permanent harm to ourselves or our civilization if we occasionally make a judgment on a book which later generations, freed from the particular situation that misled us, will have to reverse. But we do harm if we avoid taking the risk.

There is another kind of error that is hard to avoid in estimating new works. It is often difficult to see new techniques for what they really are: imagining that they are intended for old techniques, we may misread them and so consider confused or awkward what is really highly effective if approached in the proper way. Here experience with older literature will not necessarily help us—it may in fact lead us astray by conditioning us to expect a conventional technique when the writer has used a new one. To distinguish a genuine new technique from a fraudulent one, and to find a standard for making such a distinction, are among the most difficult tasks of criticism. Here again the "innocent eye" will help more than an elaborate scholarly apparatus: we must learn to see the work for what it is, not for what we might have expected it to be. There is the further danger, once we have learned to appreciate the new technique, of refusing any merit to the old. There is a kind of snobbery to be found among modern criticism which is really less forgivable than the inability to appreciate the new, for it is less likely to be honest. Not to appreciate Auden because we have been brought up on Keats is understandable if not laudable, but to refuse all merit to, say, Arnold's "Dover Beach" because we have come to like Hopkins suggests simply a desire to be "advanced." There are all sorts of affectations threatening the integrity of criticism, and the desire for modernity is not the least of them. We must learn to steer a middle path between a critical hardening of the arteries, which comes from too long dwelling in one area of past literature, and the enthusiasm for what is new and different for its own sake to which the desire to avoid the former fault sometimes leads.

CHAPTER X

Epilogue

THERE are no easy answers to any of the questions that really matter. In the foregoing pages there has been no attempt to preach any gospel; the attempt has been rather to indicate lines of thought which might help the reader to see more clearly into the function and value of literature. The more important a subject is, the less dogmatically it can be discussed: there is no single "right" theory of literature any more than there is a single "right" analysis of *Hamlet*. This does not mean that we must take refuge in airy relativism. The reason why there are no final answers to the fundamental questions is not that values do not exist, but that they are both more subtle and more comprehensive than any individual approach can master. It is true that there are right and wrong kinds of approach, right and wrong sorts of effort, but if the subject is really worth discussing even the best answers can touch on only one facet of it. The temptation to isolate one's favorite facet and then treat it as the whole is natural, and that we should succumb to it is both inevitable and proper. For if we were to wait until we could see all relevant facets at once, we should never think at all. To the eye of God, as it were, everything is relevant in discussing anything, and since the values of literature exist because experience itself has value and *quality*, there must be some ultimate relation between aesthetics, ethics, and metaphysics, between art and politics, between value in art and value in life. But it is not the simple relation sought by naïve seekers after influences and causes. Dr. Johnson wrote *Rasselas* in order to raise money to pay for his mother's funeral; Keats's genius matured early because he had tuberculosis; but these facts tell us nothing whatever about the quality of *Rasselas* or the worth of Keats's poems. The superficial conditions which seem to have "produced" a work of art have no necessary connection with its value. Ultimately, there is a connection; if we knew enough, we could perhaps see a relation between value in the cause and value in the effect; but in the present state of understanding of the human mind and its physical and social environment we must be content to make a separation between genetic and normative criticism, between questions of origin and of value, even though we may know theoretically that they must have an ultimate dependence on each other.

One thing, however, we can say. If we consider literature to be worth while, it must be because we assume that in some sense human experience is worth while and that insight into it is valuable for its own sake. But it should be said again that this does not commit us to an optimistic view of human nature. We are left free to lay stress on original sin with the Christian tradition or on original virtue ("the merits of the fathers") with the Hebrew tradition or to take neither view and consider man neither infected nor benefited by the past of the race. Or we may prefer a combination of the first two attitudes. But if we take a serious interest in imaginative literature in the sense in which it has been defined here we are committed to some kind of humanism, to some belief in the value of man's experience. If we have no such belief, why should we bother about an activity whose function is—to put the matter at its simplest—to illuminate, interpret, and give a deeper understanding of that experience? If literature is merely pattern, and not pattern put at the service of the communication of insight into man's destiny, then it is a trivial pastime which does not justify our spending too much attention on it. If, on the other hand, literature is important only to the extent that it provides allegories with a simple moral, then it is something for children and for weak-minded adults who cannot obtain instruction in morality more directly. But if, as these pages have tried to show, it is a unique way of communicating unique insights into the nature of human experience, then it is of value only if we believe that that experience is itself important and worth illuminating. Only a humanist philosophy can, in the last analysis, provide a valid aesthetic.

One need not restrict the meaning of humanism to the use of the term made by official humanist critics such as Irving Babbitt and Paul Elmer More. The term is used here in a wider sense, and in a more literal sense. Our only axiom is that man, as a "doing and suffering" creature, is interesting, is worth contemplating and trying to understand, and that his experience is significant for us because it is his experience and for no other reason. The implication is, of course, that our interest in human experience is the interest of fellow men, not of gods or angels. All human experience is potentially our experience, and that makes tragedy possible: it is also potentially our neighbors' experience, and that makes comedy possible.

The reader will have noted that we have not discussed traditional categories such as tragedy and comedy, though it would have been pleasant to do so. Nor has any attempt been made to treat all literary *genres*. Nothing has been said about drama and the relation of the acted to the written play, though frequently reference has been made to Shakespeare as a writer of fiction in the widest sense of the term. A more general approach has been preferred, in an attempt to throw some light on the nature of literary value as such. On such a foundation it would, one may hope, be possible to construct theories of tragedy and comedy and to build any number of minor categories. It seemed more important to inquire into first principles. In our time there have been many notable contributors to the superstructure of criticism, but we cannot help feeling—as a result of reading contemporary criticism and of discussing these points with students—that the ultimate bases of criticism have been too often taken for granted. Such writers as have produced philosophies of literature have tended to dissociate their inquiry too completely from practical criticism, so that their theories remain theories which the reader finds difficulty in testing by his own reading. I. A. Richards, for example, whose *Principles of Literary Criticism* was a noble structure which has had great influence, himself found difficulty in applying his general theory, as any reader of his *Practical Criticism* will observe. Perhaps the same charge will be brought against the present work: but at least an attempt has been made to treat the subject in such a way that the implications for practical criticism and literary appreciation are always apparent.

It is not always true that one must have a conscious theory of literary value before one can fully appreciate works of literature. One has only to cast one's eye back over the history of criticism to see that there have been many sensitive lovers of great literature whose views of the nature of literature seem to us crude and childish. Nevertheless, self-consciousness is a good quality in a civilization, and introspection into the nature of our intellectual pleasures often increases them (one would not make the same claim for nonintellectual pleasures). Further, when popular ideas about the nature and value of literature are as confused as they are today, and when there is a large semiliterate reading public fed with books by a commercial machine, the critic feels an obligation to clarify the main principles of literary value if only to explain to himself what has gone wrong and what ought to be right.

The trouble with an age which has a rich cultural heritage behind it is that it tends to take complacently for granted those values which in former ages were the subject of passionate debate. Even those who have no real interest in or understanding of literature are willing to assume that there is something in it, that somewhere there are its appointed guardians who look after it and know what they are doing and why they are doing it. There are, of course, no such appointed guardians. Values which everybody takes for granted soon cease to be values. If only the philistines were more militant, were more honest in openly championing their own tastes and preferences, we should know where we were and the fundamental questions would get frequent airings. The reading public are the only real guardians of literature, and, if they are so sunk in sloth that they will not even defend their prejudices, all we can hope for is that professional critics should, by attacking those prejudices, bring them out into the open and stimulate counterstatements from any who care to make them. As Matthew Arnold once remarked, quoting Bishop Wilson: "The number of those who need to be awakened is far greater than that of those who need comfort."

There are people—a growing number these days—who attack all such discussion as the foregoing because it refers to values in a civilization that is already passing away. The new world which is stirring, the new "cultural emergence" which is to come from great mass movements in Asia and from the awakening of colonial peoples, will soon render our preoccupation with literature academic and meaningless. We have every sympathy with any movement which will help to produce new cultural patterns among peoples who hitherto have had the dregs of other cultures thrust upon them, but it is difficult to see why such sympathy should absolve us from the necessity of inquiring into the nature and value of the kind of literature which Western culture has produced. If Western culture is on its way out, surely it is better to examine it now than to wait for archaeologists and anthropologists to reconstruct hypothetical fragments of it after the deluge. We are, it is sometimes argued, living in a Silver Age: if we are, surely this is the time to take stock, to inquire into and assess the values which our civilization has produced. How much less would we know of Greece and Rome if the Alexandrians and Silver Age Latin writers had not taken pains to clarify the picture for us!

But we must not approach literary values as undertakers or stocktakers. The fact that we consider them to be values means that it is our responsibility to work for their survival. If we really are living on the brink of civilization's collapse —and too many ages have believed themselves in that position to allow us to accept such a view lightly—let us reflect on what we have achieved and what we want to try to preserve. If, on the other hand, we feel that now is the time to set about planning a Brave New World, we surely have a responsibility to decide what we should take with us from the old.

‡ INDEX ‡

Index

INDEX

INDEX

In the Norton Library

CRITICISM AND THE HISTORY OF IDEAS